# CHRISTINA
# ROSSETTI

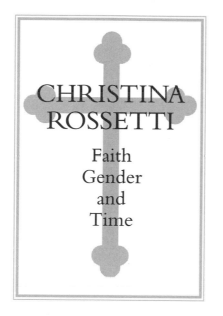

# CHRISTINA ROSSETTI

## Faith
## Gender
## and
## Time

DIANE D'AMICO

LOUISIANA STATE UNIVERSITY PRESS
*Baton Rouge*

Designer: G. Weston
Typeface: Bembo
Typesetter: Coghill Composition
Printer and binder: Thomson-Shore, Inc.

A brief excerpt from the unpublished memoirs of Sister Caroline Mary of All Saints Convent in Oxford is reproduced by permission of the All Saints Archives. Portions of some chapters herein have appeared in different form in several previously published articles and essays: part of Chapter 1 as "Christina Rossetti's 'Maude': A Reconsideration," *University of Dayton Review* 15 (spring 1981): 131–43; Chapter 2 as "'Choosing the stairs that mount above': Christina Rossetti and the Anglican Sisterhoods," *Essays in Literature* 17 (fall 1990): 204–17; Chapter 4 as "'Equal before God': Christina Rossetti and the Fallen Women of Highgate Penitentiary," in *Gender and Discourse in Victorian Literature and Art,* ed. Antony H. Harrison and Beverly Taylor, copyright © 1992 by Northern Illinois University Press; part of Chapter 5 as "Christina Rossetti's 'Helpmeet,'" *Victorian Newsletter* (spring 1994): 24–29; and part of Chapter 5 as "Eve, Mary, and Mary Magdalene: Christina Rossetti's Feminine Triptych," in *The Achievement of Christina Rossetti,* ed. David A. Kent, copyright © 1987 by Cornell University, used by permission of the publisher, Cornell University Press. Grateful acknowledgment is made to the various editors and publishers who gave permission to reprint.

Library of Congress Cataloging-in-Publication Data
D'Amico, Diane, 1951–
    Christina Rossetti : faith, gender, and time / Diane D'Amico.
    p.  cm.
    Includes bibliographical references and index.
    ISBN 0-8071-2375-7 (cloth : alk. paper)
    1. Rossetti, Christina Georgina, 1830–1894—Criticism and
interpretation.   2. Christianity and literature—England—
History—19th century.   3. Women and literature—England—
History—19th century.   4. Rossetti, Christina Georgina, 1830–1894—
Religion.   5. Christian poetry, English—History and criticism.
6. Faith in literature.   I. Title.
PR5238.D35  1999
821'.8—dc21                                              99-28005
                                                             CIP

*For*
BILL

# CONTENTS

# ACKNOWLEDGMENTS

MY THANKS AND GRATITUDE GO FIRST TO MY HUSBAND, BILL DeLamarter, for his constant interest in my work, for his thoughtful comments on the manuscript in its various stages, and especially for his willingness to talk with me about Rossetti and the issues of faith, gender, and time. Bill's own work in the field of social psychology has enhanced my perception of Rossetti as a Victorian woman of faith.

I would also like to thank Antony H. Harrison, David A. Kent, and Marjorie Stone for reading and commenting on individual chapters. I am especially grateful to Suzanne Bunkers for her careful reading of the whole manuscript. Thanks also go to Glenn Holland for his help with the interpretation of various biblical texts, to Glennis Stephenson for her helpful responses to my questions about Letitia Landon, to May Porco for her genuine interest in Rossetti's poetry and her faith, and to Frances Thomas for so many enjoyable chats about Rossetti.

I am also grateful to both the president and the dean of Allegheny College for granting me the National Endowment for the Humanities Chair (1994–1997), an appointment that gave me the time to write this book. I would like to extend a special thank-you to the staff of the Allegheny College library, especially Cynthia Burton, Don Vrabel, and Jane Westenfeld, for their patience and skill in helping me with numerous interlibrary loan requests over the years. Finally, I would like to thank the Allegheny computing staff, particularly David Anderson, for help with numerous and various computer questions and problems.

# ABBREVIATIONS OF
# ROSSETTI'S WORKS

AD    *Annus Domini: A Prayer for Each Day of the Year*

CP    *The Complete Poems of Christina Rossetti,* ed. Rebecca W. Crump, 3 vols.

CS    *Called to Be Saints: The Minor Festivals Devotionally Studied*

FD    *The Face of the Deep: A Devotional Commentary on the Apocalypse*

LS    *Letter and Spirit: Notes on the Commandments*

M    *Maude: Prose and Verse,* ed. R. W. Crump

SF    *Seek and Find: A Double Series of Short Studies of the Benedicite*

TF    *Time Flies: A Reading Diary*

# EDITORIAL NOTE

The titles of Rossetti's poems are handled in the following manner: Where Rossetti was known to have titled a poem, that title is used, and is capitalized according to modern norms. For untitled poems, I have adopted the first line of the poem as the title, maintaining Rossetti's sometimes idiosyncratic capitalization style. Single-within-double quotation marks indicate that the first line of a poem is a phrase placed in quotation marks by Rossetti—often a passage from the Bible.

# CHRISTINA
# ROSSETTI

# INTRODUCTION

## ROSSETTI
## The Woman, the Poet,
## and the Critics

For the voice is inseparable from the person
to whom it belongs. The voice which charms one
generation is inaccessible to the next.
—CHRISTINA ROSSETTI, *Time Flies*

IN *TIME FLIES: A READING DIARY,* CHRISTINA ROSSETTI REFLECTS
on the inextricable qualities of person and voice. Ironically, her reflections now read as a prediction of the critical response to her poetic voice.
For although each generation of critics has listened, with varying degrees
of interest, to that voice, the resulting descriptions of her person are contradictory. Qualities that charmed one generation were found unappeal-
ing by the next. Popular in her time as reflecting the values of a Victorian
woman of faith, her poetic voice became inaccessible to the next generation.

For the first generation of critics, those of the late Victorian period
and early decades of the twentieth century, Rossetti is viewed as a woman
of great humility whose poetry reveals the invisible world of her Christian faith. For those writing during the mid-twentieth century, she is either the repressed morbid woman whose poetry reveals sexual frustration
or an unintellectual woman whose poetry is mostly sweet sound without
sense. Most recently, she is a highly intelligent woman in a patriarchal
society whose poetry reveals both victimization and subversive feminism.
These differing images of Rossetti suggest how each generation has
sought to make her voice accessible to a different age with differing cultural and literary values. Yet such contradictory images raise several questions: Is one image of Rossetti somehow more true than the others? Are
some critics simply wrong and others right? Are we therefore to assume
that each generation had access to some truth a preceding generation
foolishly overlooked? What image or images of her life as a woman and

poet can best serve as a guide to reading her more than one thousand poems? To answer such questions, we first need to explore separately these shifting images and their origins.

The first image, that of the saintly writer of highly respected poetry, began to form during Rossetti's lifetime and took its full shape shortly after her death. In numerous articles appearing soon after she died in December 1894, her poetry is praised for both its "clear and pellucid style," and its "spiritual vision." The literary critic and poet Arthur Symons, writing for the *Saturday Review*, even goes so far as to declare her to be "among the great poets of the nineteenth century." Such praise is echoed throughout the early years of the twentieth century. In his reminiscences, the critic Edmund Gosse, for example, speaks of Rossetti as "one of the most perfect poets of the age," and although he did not share her devout faith, he nevertheless describes her as a "great saint." In these early commentaries, assessments of Rossetti's life are often interwoven with the evaluation of her poetry, especially in regard to matters of her Christian faith. Even her secular verse is read as alluding to the invisible world of the spirit: "Over all she touches there is the veil as of something spiritual."[1]

Significantly, there is general agreement among this first generation of Rossetti critics that the poet's life was one of great value precisely because of this faith. Even when writers of that time speak of her refusal of two marriage proposals for religious reasons—information made public by her brother William Michael Rossetti shortly after her death—these refusals are seen by some as further proof of her spiritual "greatness." And when this information is used not to paint the portrait of a saint but to prove that although unmarried, Rossetti "loved in a woman's way," Rossetti nevertheless remains a person to admire, even an exemplar for girls to follow. In 1898, in the *Girl's Own Paper,* a brief biography of Rossetti is set before young female readers as a form of "biographical guidance," for despite the "shadows" of her life, one of them being the fact

---

1. "Obituary: Miss Christina Rossetti," *London Times,* January 1, 1895, 4; James Ashcroft Noble, *Impressions and Memories* (London: Dent, 1895), 64; [Arthur Symons], "Christina Rossetti," *Saturday Review,* January 5, 1895, 6; Edmund Gosse, "Christina Rossetti," *Critical Kit-Kats* (1913; rpr., St. Clair Shore, Mich.: Scholarly Press, 1971), 137, 162; Alexander H. Japp, "Two Pairs of Modern Poets," *Cassell's Family Magazine* 12 (February 1895): 227.

she did not marry, she kept an "open mind and heart" and achieved a "noble contentment."[2]

As one follows Rossetti's reputation through the early decades of this century, however, a radical change occurs. The next generation of critics still follows the tradition of reading the life and the poetry as interwoven, but they tend to arrive at completely different conclusions. In a 1936 survey of British authors, for example, the entry on Rossetti goes so far as to suggest that readers see in her rejection of the marriage proposals signs of a "terror of sexual love and the responsibilities of adult life." By 1940, the scholar F. L. Lucas, while considering Rossetti worthy of selection for *Ten Victorian Poets* (she is the only woman included), finds in her poetry evidence that she was "self-doomed to sorrow," and in graphic language, Lucas speaks of Rossetti hammering "nails" into "her own flesh," concluding that "the fate of Christina Rossetti is a thing to shudder at."[3] By the mid-twentieth century, the woman once respected for both the quality of her poetry and the sincerity of her faith has definitely become the frustrated, self-tormented woman whose poems reveal a fear of her sexuality. Clearly, as Rossetti's life loses its value, especially in the eyes of the critics, so does her poetry. Poetry once read for both its aesthetic and spiritual value is read during these years as evidence of neurotic womanhood.

Such a transformation has several and at times interrelated causes. Certainly, the twentieth-century popularity of psychoanalytic theory, especially during the 1920s and 1930s, and the changing attitudes toward religion, especially expressions of an orthodox Christian faith, combine to play a part in altering Rossetti's image and place in literary history. Yet the revival of interest, occurring in the 1930s, in the metaphysical poets and shortly thereafter the discovery of Gerard Manley Hopkins, along with the continued regard for these poets, indicate that the religious subject matter of poetry did not and does not in itself prevent some form of

---

2. See, for example, Katherine Tynan, "Santa Christina," *Bookman* 41, (January 1912): 189; Elizabeth Parker, "The Love Affairs of Christina Rossetti," *University Magazine* 18 (April 1919): 255; Isabella Fyvie Mayo, "Christina Rossetti: An Appreciation," *Girl's Own Paper*, March 12, 1898, 370, 372.

3. *British Authors of the Nineteenth Century*, ed. Stanley Kunitz and Howard Haycraft (New York: H. W. Wilson, 1936), 531; F. L. Lucas, *Ten Victorian Poets* (Cambridge: Cambridge University Press, 1940), 123, 126, 130.

critical appreciation among twentieth-century scholars. It is not unusual to find such poets as Herbert and Hopkins praised throughout much of this century as Rossetti was previously, and significantly, the fact of Hopkins' celibate life as a Jesuit priest appears in no way to diminish the perceived power of his poetry. Rossetti, however, despite the occasional objection raised by a scholar of Victorian religious poetry, is repeatedly portrayed throughout the middle decades of this century as a weak woman who suffered from, as one of the major anthologies of Victorian poetry phrased it, "the terrors of her religion" and the "frustration of her womanhood."[4]

Central to understanding the reasons for Rossetti's loss of value in the literary marketplace during these years is her "womanhood." Ironically, although Victorian society defined true womanhood in terms of one's status as a wife and mother, an unmarried woman who dutifully cared for her elderly relatives and piously turned to God was still seen as having lived a meaningful life. Many even considered Rossetti to be a woman whose poetry and prose offered valuable guidance. A prose version of her most famous poem, "Goblin Market," retitled "The Good Sister," is included in *Heroines of Poetry,* a 1902 collection aimed at a young female audience. And excerpts from her devotional prose can be found in a 1904 collection for an adult audience, *A Little Book of Heavenly Wisdom: Selections from the Writings of Some English Prose Mystics.* (She is one of only four women included.) In contrast, the second generation of Rossetti critics views this unmarried woman writer as a person to analyze and perhaps pity, but not admire. Most certainly, she is not a writer to whom one should turn for guidance or comfort. Rather, for those employing a psychoanalytic approach, both Rossetti's life and poetry are to be read as warnings, especially for women writers. Implied in these various Freudian assessments of "frustrated womanhood" and "self-doomed" sorrow is the message that remaining a spinster not only limits a woman's personal

4. *Victorian Poetry and Poetics,* ed. Walter E. Houghton and G. Robert Stange (Boston: Houghton Mifflin, 1968), 600. For a questioning of this biographical approach, see Hoxie Neale Fairchild, *Religious Trends in English Poetry,* vol. 4 (New York: Columbia University Press, 1957), 302–16; Raymond Chapman, *Faith and Revolt: Studies in the Literary Influence of the Oxford Movement* (London: Weidenfeld & Nicolson, 1970), 170–307; and G. B. Tennyson, *Victorian Devotional Poetry: The Tractarian Mode* (Cambridge: Harvard University Press, 1981), 202–203.

happiness but also harms her creativity. Thus, whereas the psychoanalytic perspective encourages readers to look beyond the surface of Rossetti's poetry for underlying motives that might enrich a reading of her verse, the emphasis on sexual motivation diminishes both the value of her life and the power of her poetry.

To see the extent of this diminishment, one needs to return to the Victorian view. Although the Victorians did evaluate men and women poets differently, tending to view the poetess as belonging to an inferior order, the feminine voice, that is, a voice heard as melodic and sweet with a minimum of intellectual substance, had a respected place in Victorian literature when such a poetic voice was employed by a woman, even an unmarried woman. And it is for that very voice that Rossetti was at times ranked above her only woman rival, Elizabeth Barrett Browning, who was often judged by the Victorians as having unfortunately attempted a masculine tone of boldness. In contrast, Rossetti was heard as having assumed a passive—what Paul Elmer More, writing in the early years of this century, refers to as a "surrendering"—response to life, which he views as entirely positive, especially for a woman poet and especially when that woman is writing on religious subjects: "I have likened the artlessness of much of her writing to the sweet monotony of an aeolian harp. The comparison returns as expressing also the purely feminine spirit of her inspiration. There is in her a passive surrender to the powers of life, a religious acquiescence, which wavers between a plaintive pathos and a sublime exultation of faith."[5] Once the image of the frustrated woman replaces the Victorian image of the humble woman of faith, such high praise of the feminine disappears from Rossetti scholarship.

One might expect that the reign of the New Criticism, with its claim of ignoring all but the text, would have altered the psychoanalytic view of Rossetti, which depended so much on biographical information, and thus removed issues of womanhood from evaluations of her poetry. However, the major proponents of the New Criticism were not interested in Rossetti, and thus the psychoanalytic view of her remained largely unchallenged. Moreover, despite the claim by those embracing New Criticism that they focus only on the poetic text, the language of

<hr>

5. Paul Elmer More, "Christina Rossetti," *Atlantic Monthly* 94 (December 1904): 817.

the New Critics often reveals that the poem is being viewed through the lens of gender. Poetry that is seen to be of high value is that which is considered in form and content to be bold, original, daring, questioning, and aggressive. In other words, New Criticism privileges the traditional construction of masculinity.[6] Perhaps also, disregard for what is perceived as feminine is in part the result of the impact of psychoanalytic literary theory. In any case, whatever the cause of the masculine bias of the New Criticism, the seemingly passive and surrendering poetic voice of Rossetti draws little interest during the reign of New Critical theory. And when a critic strongly influenced by this period of scholarship does devote attention to analyzing her lyric voice in any detail, the pejorative attitude toward the feminine remains quite apparent. In 1971, Stuart Curran concludes that Rossetti is a "gifted minor" poet—a minor poet, not a great one—precisely because her voice is too feminine. Although Curran insists that for Rossetti, "God is the all-embracing fact," he concludes that as a poet she is too passive before Him to be a great poet:

> Humble and submissive; entirely unpretentious. But a great poet cannot be unpretentious: he dares and questions; he attempts to answer, not only in matters of the human being and his universe but in the less glamourous matters of diction and meter, of dramatic imagery and formal necessities. . . . [Rossetti] is neither an intellectual nor an imaginative woman, for the most part, but she has the not inconsiderable gift of felicitous music. She falls back on pretty language, the bane of so many women poets. . . . This woman's tone is too often merely effeminate, weak and nebulous. She is a good poet, an able poet, but not a great one.[7]

Where the late Victorians found Rossetti's feminine voice a major sign of her greatness, that same voice becomes a sign of her minor status.

Whether Rossetti's poetry is indeed passive and unintellectual is de-

6. For a discussion of the "aggressive *maleness*" of the New Criticism, see Jerome J. McGann, "The Religious Poetry of Christina Rossetti," *Critical Inquiry* 10 (September 1983): 127–43. See also my article "Reading and Rereading George Herbert and Christina Rossetti," *John Donne Journal* 4 (1985): 269–89.

7. Stuart Curran, "The Lyric Voice of Christina Rossetti," *Victorian Poetry* 9 (autumn 1971): 298.

batable, as are the underlying literary values that define such characteristics as signs of inferior poetry. Even this brief examination of Rossetti's transformation from a great saintly poet to merely an "able" poet indicates that literary values and tastes change, even reverse themselves entirely. However, the sharp contrast between the Victorian and the modern evaluation of Rossetti's poetic voice suggests that unless a critic was willing to argue that Rossetti's poetry was indeed original and bold, in other words, to argue that it did indeed embody traditional masculine characteristics, then Rossetti was going to remain for the twentieth-century reader a decidedly marginal figure.

Not surprisingly, therefore, when the second major transformation of Rossetti's image occurs and a reassessment of her literary value begins, in the late 1970s and early 1980s, one finds that references to the feminine appear less often. In other words, references to those qualities traditionally identified as feminine, such as passivity and submissiveness, are less frequently applied to either her work or her life. For example, those who praise Rossetti's work do not speak of the "pretty language" of her poetry but of its "consummate craftsmanship." Significantly, as the pejorative references to the supposed femininity of her verse have diminished, Rossetti the poet has regained some of the approval she lost during the modern period. No longer is she described as a marginal figure and a minor poet; rather, she is labeled a "pivotal figure" and a "major Victorian poet."[8] Similarly, Rossetti the woman is also described as a woman to respect, not pity. However, this most recent incarnation of woman and poet differs considerably from the Rossetti of the Victorians. Instead of being depicted as a woman who surrendered her soul to God, she appears as a strong-minded woman asserting the feminine self and subverting the patriarchal ideologies of her time. Because this new phase of Rossetti scholarship is a response to the preceding one, which diminished her worth, in part, by focusing on the feminine as inadequate, it is not surprising that critics who see Rossetti as a poet worthy of serious and prolonged attention avoid any reference to passivity and weakness. Yet in this most recent phase of Rossetti scholarship, the focus is still on Rosset-

---

8. David A. Kent, ed., *The Achievement of Christina Rossetti* (Ithaca: Cornell University Press, 1987), ix; Antony H. Harrison, *Christina Rossetti in Context* (Chapel Hill: University of North Carolina Press, 1988), 63.

ti's life as a woman, as it was for the Victorians and the moderns, only now womanhood is seen in different terms. For example, instead of renouncing marriage for the sake of her faith, Rossetti is seen to have been "resisting" marriage for the sake of her poetry.[9]

For those familiar with literary theory, it is obvious that this image of Rossetti as resisting and asserting is shaped by the woman's movement of the 1970s and the 1980s and the feminist literary theory associated with it. Those engaged in this reconsideration of Rossetti have been influenced by a variety of literary theories, but feminist theory has had the most influence.[10] Yet even though feminist theory has helped rescue Rossetti from the margins of literary history and rendered her poetry and her life more accessible to the current generation, the various feminist readings of Rossetti indicate signs of uneasiness with the fact of her spinsterhood, particularly if that spinsterhood is seen in terms of lifelong virginity, and especially with the fact of her Christian faith.

Feminist criticism on Rossetti and her faith can be divided into four general categories. First, there are those who, when combining feminist theory with psychoanalysis, draw connections between female creativity and female sexuality. These critics are thus inclined to see Rossetti's faith very much as the modernists did, that is, as a sign of sexual frustration, and this frustration is then seen to damage her creative impulses. Not surprisingly, therefore, the language used by such critics is strikingly reminiscent of that employed by the critics of the 1930s and the 1940s. Recently, Germaine Greer, for example, claims that Rossetti "used the aspirations of piety as a metaphor for her own frustrated sexuality" and that ultimately, she "crushed herself more efficiently than anyone else could have."[11]

Another feminist perspective resists such readings by questioning the assumption that creativity and sexuality are connected. Kathleen Blake's

9. For the image of Rossetti resisting marriage, see Pamela Norris, ed., *Sound the Deep Waters: Woman's Romantic Poetry in the Victorian Age* (Boston: Little, Brown, 1991), 118.

10. For a detailed list of Rossetti scholarship in recent years, see Jane Addison, "Christina Rossetti Studies, 1974–1991: A Checklist and Synthesis," *Bulletin of Bibliography* 2 (March 1995): 73–93.

11. Germaine Greer, *Slip-Shod Sibyls: Recognition, Rejection, and the Woman Poet* (New York: Viking, 1995), 360, 364.

work on Victorian women and "self-postponement" offers the best example of this alternate view.[12] In this reading, Rossetti's faith appears not as a repressive force that stifles creativity but as a subject that provides material for poetry, especially since Rossetti was a woman. In other words, Blake's emphasis is on Rossetti the woman poet who makes art out of her condition as a Victorian woman, and that condition, according to Blake, resembles that of a Christian waiting for fulfillment. In this reading, Rossetti's faith is not presented as harmful to poetic creativity, and yet her faith remains subordinate to her Victorian womanhood.

A third perspective tends to present Rossetti's faith as a device for overcoming the difficulty of being a woman in Victorian England. For example, Dolores Rosenblum argues that "religious experience" offers a woman poet "legitimized ways of imagining recognition and restitution" in a world that oppresses her. Angela Leighton, in her more recent study of Victorian woman poets, offers a reading that shares this approach: Leighton sees Rossetti as more interested in the world of imagination than the spiritual world, for in fantasy she could experience a kind of freedom. Leighton claims that "at some level," Rossetti was "profoundly indifferent to both love and faith."[13] Finally, feminist readings have been offered that either ignore Rossetti's faith or give it little attention.[14]

Although feminist theory has expanded our understanding of what it meant to be a woman poet in Victorian England and thus drawn our attention to the ways in which Rossetti's poetry both reflects and responds to that situation, feminist scholarship has yet to explore in any detail Rossetti's faith as an essential part of that situation. In a sense, we have not yet allowed Rossetti to be a woman poet of faith. Comparing those critical readings of Rossetti's "'The Heart Knoweth Its Own Bitterness'" that were written before feminist theory began to change the literary landscape with more recent readings will help make this point.

12. Kathleen Blake, *Love and the Woman Question in Victorian Literature: The Art of Self-Postponement* (Totowa, N.J.: Barnes and Noble, 1983), ix.

13. Dolores Rosenblum, *Christina Rossetti: The Poetry of Endurance* (Carbondale, Ill.: Southern Illinois University Press, 1986), 16; Angela Leighton, *Victorian Women Poets: Writing Against the Heart* (Charlottesville: University Press of Virginia, 1992), 163, 159.

14. See, for example, Sharon Leder with Andrea Abbott, *The Language of Exclusion: The Poetry of Emily Dickinson and Christina Rossetti* (Westport, Conn.: Greenwood Press, 1987). Leder and Abbott offer an insightful reading of Rossetti's work within the socio-historical context; however, little attention is given to Rossetti's faith.

Composed in 1857, "'The Heart Knoweth Its Own Bitterness'" was not published until after Rossetti's death, when William Michael Rossetti included it in *New Poems* (1896). (Rossetti herself published, in *Time Flies,* a much-revised version of the poem, discussed in chapter 6.) As is typical of many of Rossetti's poems, the speaker of "'The Heart Knoweth'" finds the things of this world inadequate and looks to heaven for full satisfaction:

When all the over-work of life
   Is finished once, and fast asleep
We swerve no more beneath the knife
   But taste that silence cool and deep;
Forgetful of the highways rough,
   Forgetful of the thorny scourge,
   Forgetful of the tossing surge,
Then shall we find it is enough?—

How can we say "enough" on earth;
   "Enough" with such a craving heart:
I have not found it since my birth
   But still have bartered part for part.
I have not held and hugged the whole,
   But paid the old to gain the new;
   Much have I paid, yet much is due,
Till I am beggared sense and soul.

I used to labour, used to strive
   For pleasure with a restless will:
Now if I save my soul alive
   All else what matters, good or ill?
I used to dream alone, to plan
   Unspoken hopes and days to come:—
   Of all my past this is the sum:
I will not lean on child of man.

To give, to give, not to receive,
   I long to pour myself, my soul,

Not to keep back or count or leave
   But king with king to give the whole:
I long for one to stir my deep—
   I have had enough of help and gift—
   I long for one to search and sift
Myself, to take myself and keep.

You scratch my surface with your pin;
   You stroke me smooth with hushing breath;—
Nay pierce, nay probe, nay dig within,
   Probe my quick core and sound my depth.
You call me with a puny call,
   You talk, you smile, you nothing do;
   How should I spend my heart on you,
My heart that so outweighs you all?

Your vessels are by much too strait;
   Were I to pour you could not hold,
Bear with me: I must bear to wait
   A fountain sealed thro' heat and cold.
Bear with me days or months or years;
   Deep must call deep until the end
   When friend shall no more envy friend
Nor vex his friend at unawares.

Not in this world of hope deferred,
   This world of perishable stuff;—
Eye hath not seen, nor ear hath heard,
   Nor heart conceived that full "enough":
Here moans the separating sea,
   Here harvests fail, here breaks the heart;
   There God shall join and no man part,
I full of Christ and Christ of me.

                                  (*CP,* 3:265–66)

Critics writing during the prefeminist period of Rossetti scholarship
find in this poem evidence that Rossetti was a woman of suppressed sex-

ual passions who achieved self-control only after a long and difficult battle. For example, Mary Sandars, in her 1930 biography of the poet, reads the poem as a sign that "Christina, tired and irritated, was giving way to feelings suppressed in her controlled moments with an iron hand." Lucas, in her 1940 book on Victorian poets, finds proof that behind Rossetti's quiet exterior there was "passion to be mastered." Although occasional mention is made of the religious nature of the poem, none of this early commentary focuses on sacred love as the poem's theme. Lucas, moreover, by concluding that Rossetti was "born to have been one of the great lovers of history," implies that erotic love is the poem's main subject. A more recent critic, Georgina Battiscombe, gives some attention to Rossetti's belief in God, yet she too reads the poem as a personal document revealing an "unconscious sublimation of sex."[15] All these readings show to some extent the influence of the psychoanalytic school of Rossetti criticism, and all read the "I" of the poem as Rossetti herself.

The most recent criticism on the poem shows primarily the influence of feminist theory. Thus, there is a slight shift from presenting Rossetti as the sexually repressed woman struggling with her passions to presenting her as a woman who is oppressed by patriarchy and who is questioning that oppression in this poem. For example, Barbara Garlick reads "'The Heart Knoweth'" as Rossetti's reaction to the limited view of womanhood to be found in the paintings of the Pre-Raphaelite Brotherhood. Jan Marsh, Rossetti's most recent biographer, concludes, "Above all, [this poem] articulates the female sense of unfocused dissatisfaction, powered by indefinite or inadmissable cravings." Although these readings suggest that the "you" of the poem ("You talk, you smile, you nothing do") be read as referring to the whole patriarchal structure of Victorian society and not just to a male lover, these feminist readings nevertheless still focus on issues of Rossetti's womanhood. "The heart" in the title is still being read as Rossetti's heart, and the "bitterness" expressed is being read as a bitterness arising out of her situation as a woman. In recent criticism there are even slight signs of a tendency to associate the poem with what we know of Rossetti's love life. In their recently published anthol-

15. Mary F. Sandars, *The Life of Christina Rossetti* (London: Hutchinson, 1930), 125–26; Lucas, *Ten Victorian Poets,* 135, 137; Georgina Battiscombe, *Christina Rossetti: A Divided Life* (London: Constable, 1981), 130.

ogy of Victorian women poets, Angela Leighton and Margaret Reynolds suggest that perhaps this poem is in part Rossetti's response to Charles Cayley's "religious half-heartedness" and "emotional dithering."[16]

When writing this poem, Rossetti may have drawn on a disappointing romance. And her experience as an intelligent and gifted woman in a patriarchal society well might have contributed to her understanding of human bitterness. However, to read this poem primarily as the outpourings of Rossetti's heart is to overlook the poet in her and to ignore the centrality of her Christian faith. In other words, it is to overlook the distinct possibility that as a woman with a creative imagination, she well might have been trying to express not personal frustrations but the sentiments of any human being who finds the things of this world inadequate and who turns to a belief in an ideal realm of the spirit.

Indeed, Rossetti's title, which is taken directly from Prov. 14:10 ("The heart knoweth its own bitterness; and a stranger doth not intermeddle with its joy"), actually encourages such a reading. Rather than follow the King James translation, which is Rossetti's usual practice, she has turned to an alternate reading, one that uses the pronoun "its" where the Authorized version uses "his."[17] One might argue that she chose such a translation so as to better express an autobiographical impulse, but I would assert that the use of "its" suggests she was attempting a genderless expression of human sorrow and frustation. If one insists on assigning a gender to the voice of the poem, the biblical allusions actually are more suggestive of masculine voices. Proverbs is the book of the Bible in which Solomon, the son of David and king of Israel, offers advice to a younger man referred to as "son." The expression of dissatisfaction with this life strongly echoes the voice of the preacher of Ecclesiastes, also be-

---

16. Barbara Garlick, "The Frozen Fountain: Christina Rossetti, the Virgin Model, and Youthful Pre-Raphaelitism," in *Virginal Sexuality and Textuality in Victorian Literature,* ed. Lloyd Davis (Albany: State University of New York Press, 1993), 126; Jan Marsh, *Christina Rossetti: A Writer's Life* (London: Jonathan Cape, 1994), 191; Angela Leighton and Margaret Reynolds, eds., *Victorian Women Poets: An Anthology* (Oxford: Blackwell, 1995), 354.

17. Rossetti's prefatory note in *Seek and Find* indicates that she did sometimes consider translations other than the King James version: "Any textual elucidations, as I know neither Hebrew nor Greek, are simply based upon some translation; many valuable alternate readings being found in the Margin of an ordinary Reference Bible."

lieved to be Solomon. For example, compare line 51 of the poem with Eccl. 1:8: "The eye is not satisfied with seeing, nor the ear filled with hearing." Indeed, the speaker of this poem sounds much more like the weary and wise, experienced speaker of Ecclesiastes, who once sought all manner of worldly pleasures, than a twenty-seven-year-old middle-class Victorian woman.

The poem is also punctuated with echoes of the Psalms, and thus the speaker can be associated with King David. For example, the speaker's longing for one to "search and sift" parallels the voice one hears in Ps. 139: "Search me, O God, and know my heart: try me, and know my thoughts." Line 46 echoes Ps. 42:7, and line 24 ("I will not lean on child of man") is taken directly from the Book of Common Prayer version of Ps. 146:2: "O put not your trust in princes, nor in any child of man for there is no help in them." Again, it is especially significant that Rossetti uses an alternate translation as opposed to the King James version. In the King James version, the line reads as follows: "I will not lean on any son of man." By using the word *child,* which is not gender specific, Rossetti suggests that the speaker will not lean on son or daughter. The speaker of this poem is rejecting not just a patriarchal society but the world itself. When Rossetti's speaker refers to those who "scratch" only the "surface" and call with "a puny call," one might imagine that this angry speaker has in mind not just patriarchy but all those of Victorian England who seek only immediate satisfaction and focus only on the surface of life. And if one turns to this poem after reading the Psalms, one might well read those whose behavior so angers and disappoints the speaker as those referred to throughout the Psalms as the "ungodly," or those who try to corrupt through flattery the "godly man" (see, for example, Ps. 12).

Line 44, in which the speaker describes her or himself as a "fountain sealed," does associate the speaker with a woman in that it echoes the Song of Songs 4:12, a text in which the bridegroom refers to his beloved as "a spring shut up, a fountain sealed." However, if we keep in mind the religious nature of the poem, Rossetti's use of the phrase might easily be read not in terms of sexual repression or even a turning away from joy, but rather as evidence that the speaker has rejected evil and the corrupting influences of the world. Rev. Richard Frederick Littledale, an Anglican clergyman and personal friend of Rossetti's, suggests such a reading of this metaphor in his 1869 commentary on the Song of Songs: "This fountain is sealed, because the word of the Gospel creed is protected with the seal of truth, so that neither heretics nor evil spirits may be able to violate or break in upon the Catholic Faith."[18] Furthermore, if we recognize Rossetti's devout Christian faith, we read the allusion to "a fountain sealed" with the knowledge that Rossetti found in the Song of Songs not a narrative of erotic love but rather one of the sacred love between Christ and the soul. For Rossetti, the bride of the Songs of Songs was the human soul, whether that soul was housed in a male or female body. And though Rossetti employs nuptial imagery in the very last lines of the poem, again her speaker need not be seen as female. Significantly, the last line of the poem echoes both the Anglican Communion service ("then we dwell in Christ, and Christ in us; we are one with Christ and Christ with us"), and St. Paul's letter to the Ephesians, in which Paul speaks to all believers of being "filled with all the fullness of God" (see Eph. 3:19).

Reading "'The Heart Knoweth Its Own Bitterness'" within the context of its biblical sources and within the context of Rossetti's faith leads to a richer and more complex reading of the poem than that offered by Rossetti scholars to date, for it leads us to see that the "I" of the poem, the bitter speaker who turns to God, both is and is not Rossetti. Certainly, Rossetti consistently viewed this world as inadequate, and quite possibly this poem reveals some of her frustrations as a Victorian woman, whether sexual or political. However, when as a poet Rossetti employs the language of preacher, psalmist, Christian disciple, and even the language of the priest during Holy Communion, she reaches beyond herself and beyond the feminine sphere of her time. She joins her poetic voice with a chorus of biblical voices, voices that preach to others and voices that lament to God, but voices that nonetheless have power and meaning for all readers, whether male or female. It is Rossetti's faith that empowers her to speak with this authority.

In drawing such a conclusion, however, I am not claiming that the true image of Rossetti was the one offered by the Victorians. Although the Victorian critics indeed saw Rossetti as a woman of faith, and saw her poetry as a product of that faith, the saintly image they present tends to diminish her power and importance by removing her from her own

---

18. Richard Frederick Littledale, *A Commentary on the Song of Songs* (London: Joseph Masters, 1869), 180.

time; in other words, she is seen as an idealized figure responding to her god but not her age. The Victorian image of Rossetti excludes from consideration her involvement in and response to some of the controversial issues of her day, such as the establishment of Anglican sisterhoods, the treatment of fallen women, and the extension of the franchise. The Victorian assessment of Rossetti implies that her faith distanced her from such events, whereas in fact her faith involved her in those events. Nor am I suggesting that while focusing on Rossetti's faith as she practiced it in a particular historical moment, we should overlook what it meant to be a woman then. Certainly, both Rossetti's life and poetry were shaped by both the limitations and the privileges of middle-class Victorian womanhood. (For example, she was not allowed an education outside the home, as her brothers were, but neither did the primary burden of financial support for the family fall upon her, as it did her brother William Michael.)

Rather, I am suggesting that Rossetti scholars need to accept the Victorian view that Rossetti's faith was central to both her life and poetry and incorporate that view into the current interest in gender.[19] Furthermore, even though feminist critics employing a psychoanalytic approach have turned our attention to the complexity of Rossetti's inner life, such an approach has too often reduced a rich and complex body of work to the neurotic outpourings of a morbid mind. In suggesting that we follow the Victorian point of view, I am therefore also arguing that we accept Rossetti's faith, neither as evidence of sexual repression nor as absolute truth, but what is more important, as absolute truth to her.[20] Such an ac-

19. I should like to mention here a recent work that contributes significantly to Rossetti scholarship: Sharon Smulders, *Christina Rossetti Revisited* (New York: Twayne, 1996). Smulders' approach resembles mine in that we both consider issues of Rossetti's gender, time, and faith in discussions of her poetry. Our approaches differ in that Smulders places at the center of her analysis Rossetti's versatility as a writer, whereas I give more attention to Rossetti's faith.

20. During the 1990s, several articles have appeared in which Rossetti's faith is accorded serious, nonjudgmental attention. This suggests that a new trend in Rossetti scholarship is developing. See, for example, Mary Arseneau, "Pilgrimage and Postponement: Christina Rossetti's 'The Prince's Progress,'" *Victorian Poetry* 32 (autumn–winter 1994): 279–98; Linda E. Marshall, "'Transfigured to His Likeness': Sensible Transcendentalism in Christina Rossetti's 'Goblin Market,'" *University of Toronto Quarterly* 63 (spring 1994): 429–50; and David A. Kent, "Christina Rossetti's Dying," *Journal of Pre-Raphaelite Studies* 5 (fall 1996): 83–97.

ceptance helps us better appreciate, as this book aims to show, that Rossetti's complete commitment to her Christian faith, her experience as a Victorian woman, and her poetic vocation are inextricably interwoven.

If we attempt to weave together the Victorian respect for the reality of Rossetti's faith with the recent interest in the significance of gender, we shall not see the one true Rossetti. However, we shall see a complex woman poet who changed and developed in response to her faith, her gender, and her time, and who therefore can not be easily classified as Victorian saint or frustrated woman or subversive feminist. If the current generation of Rossetti scholars seeks to imagine her in this multifaceted way, perhaps it will be less likely that Christina Rossetti's work and life will be so easily dismissed when literary tastes and values change again.

*one*

# ROSSETTI'S RESPONSE TO THE FEMININE VOICE OF WOE

✝

THE WOMAN POET OF THE EARLY DECADES OF THE NINETEENTH century was expected to follow the gender ideology of her time. That is, her poetry was to focus on the domestic sphere of home and hearth and to do so with an emphasis on feeling and emotion in sentimental and at times effusive language full of pleasing sound.[1] The careers of Felicia Hemans and Letitia Elizabeth Landon both suggest that if a woman poet met these expectations, she might be both a popular and critical success. Although Hemans is rarely read today, her work had a wide audience throughout the nineteenth century in both Britain and America. William Michael Rossetti edited a collection of her poems in 1873; more important, in the 1840s, when Christina Rossetti was developing her own poetic voice, Hemans was still ranked as "the most generally admired of all English female poets, and deservedly so."[2] Although Landon's verse was

1. See Stuart Curran, "Romantic Poetry: The Altered I," in *Romanticism and Feminism*, ed. Anne K. Mellor (Bloomington: Indiana University Press, 1988), 185–207; Glennis Stephenson, "Letitia Landon and the Victorian Improvisatrice: The Construction of L.E.L.," *Victorian Poetry* 30 (spring 1992): 1–17; and Angela Leighton, *Victorian Women Poets: Writing Against the Heart* (Charlottesville: University Press of Virginia, 1992).

2. George Bethune, *British Female Poets* (1848; rpr., New York: Books for Libraries, 1972), 188. Regarding the popularity of Hemans' poetry, see Donald H. Reiman, Introduction to *Records of Woman* (1828; rpr., New York: Garland, 1978), v.

less favorably evaluated during the 1840s than it had been when first published, her poetry still had popular appeal. As with Hemans, collections of Landon's poetry were reprinted throughout the nineteenth century.

The melancholy strain of Rossetti's early work clearly belongs to the tradition of woman's poetry characterized by Hemans and Landon. Other scholars have made note of this fact.[3] However, little attention has been given thus far to the significance of Rossetti's faith. A close comparison of Rossetti's early poems with those of these two literary foremothers does suggest that even when beginning her poetic career, Rossetti was not only imitating but also responding to the work of her female predecessors and doing so from the vantage point of her Christian faith. Although Rossetti's early poems often echo their work, suggesting that she felt these women had something to teach her, she also begins to revise and adapt what she learns to suit her purposes, which more often emphasize the religious than the romantic and begin to shift the poetic subject from a woman's heart to her soul. Moreover, while Rossetti was reading the poetry of Hemans and Landon, in a sense listening to the feminine voices of sorrow, she was also listening to voices of preachers and prophets, voices that spoke of the vanity of this life and the need to prepare for the next.

We can begin to examine this process of revision and adaptation by comparing some of Rossetti's early poetic dramatizations of woman's life with Hemans' *Records of Woman*, one of her most successful volumes.[4] *Records of Woman* is a series of monologues and lyric narratives in which individual women drawn from legend and history tell of their suffering for love. Although a few poems in the collection focus on a mother's love, most show a woman suffering as a consequence of love for husband or lover. For example, the first poem in the collection is based on the life of Arabella Stuart, who was imprisoned by King James I for a marriage he found politically dangerous to his reign, and "Costanza," placed midway in the volume, tells of a woman who fled society to live a saintly life, ministering to the sorrow of others, because the man she loved chose the

3. See, for example, Dolores Rosenblum, *Christina Rossetti: The Poetry of Endurance* (Carbondale, Ill.: Southern Illinois University Press, 1986), 1–20; and Leighton, *Victorian Women Poets*, 118–63.

4. *Dictionary of Literary Biography*, 96:139.

"gauds of pride" over his love for her. The last poem, "The Grave of a Poetess," is written in honor of the eighteenth-century poet Mary Tighe, believed by many to have had a loveless marriage. In general, the message of Hemans' *Records* appears to be that woman's lot is one of suffering caused by love, suggesting therefore that such suffering is the appropriate keynote for the woman poet.

Several of Rossetti's poems of the 1840s, especially the period 1847–1848, strike the same note of suffering, and they recall not only in tone but also in form Hemans' work. Like Hemans, Rossetti borrows from already existing narratives of women's lives and develops monologues in which the character expresses her anguish. Furthermore, even though Rossetti tends to draw her female figures from popular novels rather than history and folktales, she also repeatedly focuses on women who suffer as a consequence of unrequited or ill-fated love. "Eva" (1847) and the two poems entitled "Zara," one written 1847 and one in 1848, are based on Charles Robert Maturin's *Women: Or Pour et Contre*, the plot of which involves a mother and daughter unknowingly falling in love with the same young man. "Isidora" (1847) and "Immalee" (1847) are inspired by Maturin's novel *Melmoth the Wanderer* and refer to the female character who eventually must choose between her soul and her love for Melmoth. "Lady Montrevor" (1848) is based on a character in Maturin's *Wild Irish Boy* whose vanity traps her into marrying a man she does not love. The source of the sonnet "Ellen Middleton" (1848) is Georgina Fullerton's novel of the same name, which tells a tale of married love marred by the wife's guilty secret. "A Hopeless Case," first entitled "Nydia," (1848) is based on a character in Edward Bulwer-Lytton's *Last Days of Pompeii* who suffers from an unrequited love; "Undine" (1848) is based on a popular nineteenth-century folktale by Baron de La Motte Fouque telling of a water spirit betrayed by her mortal husband.

In these Rossettian "records of women," the speakers at times use extravagant language full of cries of longing and self-sacrifice, reminiscent of Hemans' speakers. The two Zara poems are especially Hemans-like in this regard. "Zara" (1847) is a long anguished cry of love, and hate born of love, which ends with a final self-sacrificing statement of forgiveness:

I forgive thee, dearest, cruel, I forgive thee;—
May thy cup of sorrow be poured out for me;

Though the dregs be bitter yet they shall not grieve me,
Knowing that I drink them, O my love, for thee.

(*CP*, 3:112)

In the 1848 version of Zara's monologue, she contemplates suicide because her "false friend" has wearied of her, yet even in her thoughts of suicide she still expresses the hope that the man who betrayed her will be with her after death: "Shall not we twain repose together?" (3:162). Such total devotion to the beloved recalls Hemans' faithful women who continue to love no matter the circumstances: Arabella's husband never rescues her; Juana's husband never awakes from death to love her; Costanza's lover asks forgiveness but only when he is dying; and Properzia Rossi dies because she cannot stop loving the man who has rejected her.

Both Hemans and Rossetti appear to imply that women are doomed to be disappointed because men are less capable than women of loving faithfully. Of course, this negative portrayal of the male is due in part to the source material upon which Hemans and Rossetti draw. For example, the legend associated with the Italian sculptor Properzia Rossi, according to Hemans' note, tells of her dying because the Roman knight she loved was indifferent to both her and her art, and *Women*, a novel to which Rossetti seems to have been especially drawn, depicts the male of the love triangle as easily infatuated and therefore irresponsible. Furthermore, the belief that men were less constant in love was often accepted as more than a literary convention, as Francis Jeffrey's 1829 review of *Records of Woman* indicates. When discussing what he considers the woman poet's strengths and weaknesses, he firmly states that one of women's strengths is "their capacity of noble and devoted attachment, and of the efforts and sacrifices it may require," and he affirms, in that capacity, "they are, beyond all doubt, our [men's] superiors."[5] With such a literary and cultural heritage, it is not surprising that Rossetti's female figures find romantic love disappointing; however, at times their response, in both gesture and speech, to such disappointment is markedly different from that portrayed by Hemans. Whereas the women in Hemans' *Records* do accept what the speaker in her poem "Indian Woman's

5. Francis Jeffrey, review of Hemans' *Records of Woman, Edinburgh Review* 50 (October 1829): 33.

Death Song" calls "woman's weary lot" (in other words, they do not show anger or resentment directly), Rossetti's female characters do at times act and speak in less conventionally feminine ways. That is, occasionally a Rossetti heroine refuses to weep.

The entire text of "Undine" can be read as undercutting the literary convention of the weeping, broken-hearted woman. The poem appears to begin at the moment when the water spirit fully realizes the extent of her husband's betrayal: "She did not answer him again / But walked straight to the door" (*CP,* 3:151). Undine literally turns her back on her husband, and her refusal to "answer him," her silence, can be read as an act of self-respect, if not self-assertion. Moreover, Rossetti's repeated use of the negative effectively points out that Undine is acting contrary to the traditional broken-hearted female: "Her hand nor trembled on the lock, / Nor her foot on the floor," and although her "lips grew white" when she "looked on him once more: . . . the fire / Of her eyes did not fail" (3:152). Contrary to the sentimental portrayal of woman, Rossetti's Undine does not plead or weep. Significantly, Rossetti appears to have imagined this scene in which Undine walks "straight to the door," for there is no exact parallel in Baron de La Motte Fouque's tale.

Perhaps the most striking example in these early poems of the woman who may be brokenhearted but refuses to show it can be found in the sonnet "Lady Montrevor." This poem not only indicates that Rossetti was beginning to find the image of the weeping woman unsatisfactory but also that she was beginning to find her effusive language of lost love equally problematic:

> I do not look for love that is a dream:
>     I only seek for courage to be still;
>     To bear my grief with an unbending will,
> And when I am a-weary not to seem.
> Let the round world roll on; let the sun beam;
>     Let the wind blow, and let the rivers fill
>     The everlasting sea; and on the hill
> The palms almost touch heaven, as children deem.
> And though young Spring and Summer pass away,
>     And Autumn and cold Winter come again;
>     And though my soul, being tired of its pain,

Pass from the ancient earth; and though my clay
Return to dust; my tongue shall not complain:
No man shall mock me after this my day.

(*CP*, 3:153)

In this instance, Rossetti seems to have been strongly influenced by her source, for at one point in the novel *Wild Irish Boy*, Lady Montrevor delivers a speech, the sentiment of which this sonnet partially echoes: "I will carry the anguish of a proud heart to the grave: there it is bringing me fast, and not a soul will weep upon my grave, no heart will ache for, no tongue pity me; so much the better; I only asked for admiration, and that I will have till death."[6] Significantly, however, although Rossetti is faithful to her source by indicating that her speaker is motivated by pride (she does not want the world to mock her), Rossetti's version of Lady Montrevor's voice has biblical intonations not characteristic of Maturin's character. The world-weary tones of lines 6–13 with reference to the continual and unchanging movements of the sun, wind, rivers, and sea are reminiscent of the first chapter of Ecclesiastes: "The sun also ariseth, and the sun goeth down. . . . The wind goeth toward the south and turneth about unto the north. . . . All the rivers run into the sea; yet the sea is not full." Until the last line of the sonnet, which is faithful to Rossetti's source, Lady Montrevor sounds as if she has learned the message of the preacher: "Vanity of vanities; all is vanity." This blending of an ill-fated heroine of romance with the message of Ecclesiastes indicates that by the winter of 1848, when Rossetti was still quite young, only seventeen years old, she was clearly beginning to see the image of feminine woe through the lens of her faith. In fact, the cup imagery, which figures so prominently in the concluding lines of "Zara" (1847), suggests that perhaps even a year earlier Rossetti was beginning to cast the figure of the broken-hearted woman in biblical terms. Zara's cup of sacrificial love from which she is willing to drink recalls Christ's suffering in the garden of Gethsemane.

"Ellen Middleton," composed during the spring of 1848, offers yet another, and more obvious, example of Rossetti giving a broken-hearted

6. Charles Robert Maturin, *The Wild Irish Boy*, 2 vols. (New York: D. and G. Bruce, 1808), 2:182.

woman a biblical cadence and idiom. The poem begins with the characteristic mournful tones of the dying woman:

> Raise me; undraw the curtain; that is well.
>     Put up the casement; I would see once more
>     The golden sun-set flooding sea and shore.

(CP, 3:158)

In line five, however, this mournful tone suddenly shifts to a more prophetic one:

> The tree of love a bitter fruitage bore,
>     Sweet at the rind but rotten at the core,
>     Pointing to heaven and bringing down to hell.

(3:158)

The imagery of tree and fruit brings to mind the Genesis story of the Fall
and the dire consequences of eating the fruit of the tree of the knowledge
of good and evil. In these lines, Ellen's voice evokes not so much the
image of the dying woman but rather that of a priest delivering a sermon
on Chapter 3 of Genesis. The tone of her voice and the warning of love's
dangers also bring to mind the voice of Solomon in Prov. 5:5, cautioning
the young man against the evil ways of the woman whose "steps take
hold on hell." Also echoed is the voice of Isaiah (14:12–15), in a passage
read by Christians as telling of the fall of Lucifer from heaven to hell. Finally, the last line of the poem, in which Ellen describes her life as having
been one of "hidden" faith and "vain" love, keeps the poem focused as
much on the state of her soul as her heart.

At one point in Fullerton's novel, Ellen does compare her case to various passages from Scripture, yet the language of the Bible is not characteristic of her speech, and her death scene and her last words have none
of the prophetic power of Rossetti's sonnet. In the novel, she dies as her
husband, with whom she has been reconciled, reads the Prayers for the
Dying, and her last word is simply "amen." She dies a humble repentant
wife; it is Rossetti, not Fullerton, who gives Ellen the intonations of the
Bible and thus aligns the dying woman's voice with that of the preacher.
Although Rossetti uses her sources, as Hemans does, more for establish-

ing a general situation of distress than for exact details, it is important to give these sources more than a cursory glance, for they offer further evidence that Rossetti's poetic imagination when a young woman was as much drawn to matters of the soul as it was matters of the heart.

Although Fullerton's *Ellen Middleton* is full of melodramatic love scenes, swooning fainting spells, and brain fever brought on by unrequited love, it is also about faith and guilt, especially about the need to confess. As indicated above, the novel focuses on a young woman's guilty secret: in a moment of anger she slapped her eight-year old cousin, who was teasing and tormenting her; the cousin fell down a flight of steps into the water and died before she could be saved. Ellen keeps her part in her cousin's accident a secret. For several years, and through hundreds of pages, she struggles with herself, knowing that to confess is the only way she will find peace, yet fearing she will lose her husband's love if she does. Rossetti's sonnet, with its emphasis on faith and vanity, suggests that she responded to the scenes of religious crisis as much if not more than the love scenes. Similarly, when she read Maturin's *Women,* it is quite possible she found it to be as much about religious belief as about ill-fated love. Loving the weak-willed Charles leads both Eva and Zara to a religious crisis, and Maturin devotes whole chapters to delineating their spiritual struggles. Although unsuccessful in her quest for spiritual peace, Zara tries to keep the image of the crucified savior before her as she attempts to renounce her love for Charles. Ultimately, Eva decides that in loving Charles, she was loving the world too much and that she must renounce him if she is to see God. Maturin's Isidora in *Melmoth the Wanderer* experiences a similar temptation, and although *Melmoth* is full of graphic descriptions of physical and mental suffering, Rossetti's "Isidora," with its focus on the dying woman's struggle to choose "twixt God and man," suggests again that for the young poet the greatest horror was not to lose a man's love but to lose one's soul.

At approximately the same time she was writing most of these poetic portraits of women, Rossetti was writing poems on the vanity of human life. In 1847 she wrote "Vanity of Vanities," a sonnet based, as the title suggests, on Ecclesiastes, and in 1849, "One Certainty" and "A Testimony," both echoing the same biblical message. This life and all associated with it must be seen for what it is, ephemeral and therefore of little significance. Rossetti scholars have often noted that an early theme, which came to characterize her mature poetic voice as well, was that of the vanity of earthly things.[7] Yet more attention should be given to how important her echoing of this voice of Ecclesiastes is in regard to her position as a woman poet. In looking closely at how Rossetti uses the Bible, one sees that she does not so much allude to biblical texts as adopt the voice of those texts; thus, her poetic voice takes on tones of authority not characteristic of the woman poet's sphere.

For example, the first stanza of "A Testimony" reads:

> I said of laughter: it is vain.
>   Of mirth I said: what profits it?
>   Therefore I found a book, and writ
> Therein how ease and also pain,
> How health and sickness, every one
> Is vanity beneath the sun.

(CP, 1:77)

The "I" is the author of Ecclesiastes, but in using that first-person pronoun, Rossetti, a woman poet, associates herself with the Preacher. Thus, although in the last stanza, with mention of the "King" who "dwelt in Jerusalem," Rossetti indicates that she has been writing a poetic version of Ecclesiastes, she has in a sense been speaking as if she were "the wisest man on earth" (1:78). In "One Certainty," she quotes Ecclesiastes to establish the voice of the Preacher and then weaves various biblical texts together to convey her own message:

> Vanity of vanities, the Preacher saith,
>   All things are vanity. The eye and ear
>   Cannot be filled with what they see and hear.
> Like early dew, or like the sudden breath
> Of wind, or like the grass that withereth,
>   Is man, tossed to and fro by hope and fear.

(1:72)

7. For example, see Nilda Jimenez, *The Bible and the Poetry of Christina Rossetti: A Concordance* (Westport, Conn.: Greenwood Press, 1979), x.

In lines 2–3, Rossetti alludes to St. Paul's first epistle to the Corinthians, in which he echoes Isa. 64: "Eye hath not seen, nor ear heard, neither have entered into the heart of man, the things which God hath prepared for them that love him" (1 Cor. 2:9). In line 5, Rossetti's image of withered grass recalls the complaint of Ps. 102:4: "My heart is smitten and withered like grass." Thus, in this sonnet Rossetti has linked her poetic voice with the preacher of Ecclesiastes, the prophet Isaiah, the disciple Paul, and the psalmist David. An especially important mingling of biblical voices occurs in "Vanity of Vanities," where Rossetti borrows from Rev. 8:12 to predict when the weary tones of Ecclesiastes will cease to be repeated: the "sinking heart" will continue to bemoan the vanity of earthly things until "the mighty angel-blast / Is blown, making the sun and moon aghast" (*CP*, 1:153). In these lines, the female poet chooses as her predecessor not only the wise and weary preacher of Ecclesiastes but also the visionary St. John the Divine and, in so doing, links her poetry with his prophecies.

When Rossetti began writing her religious verse, religion was seen as an especially appropriate subject for a woman poet; however, both male and female critics of the time tended to dictate certain limits. Mary Ann Stoddart, for example, in her book on female writers, while claiming a place for women in the religious realm, cautions against self-assertion: "We freely confess that there are departments of religious labour in which it is not meet and proper for a woman to enter, and more extensively than to mere oral instruction perhaps, may the words of the apostle be applied: 'I suffer not a woman to teach, nor to usurp authority over the man, but to be in silence.'" Stoddart continues, "Anything of an authoritative or a dictatorial manner is peculiarly repulsive in women at any time," because, Stoddart concludes, "the Gospel [inculcated] upon her the duties of modesty, meekness, and humility." Frederick Rowton, in his 1848 anthology of women's poetry, claims that women surpass men in the area of religion, but only in serving as models of faith, hope, and piety: "It has not now to be proved, I imagine, that in simple steadfastness of faith, in gentle calmness of hope and in sweet enthusiasm of piety, woman far surpasses man."[8] Rowton is here discussing Hemans and pre-

---

8. Mary Ann Stoddart, *Female Writers: Thoughts on Their Proper Sphere and Powers of Usefulness* (London: R. B. Seeley, 1842), 161–62; Frederic Rowton, *The Female Poets of Great Britain* (1848; rpr., Detroit: Wayne State University Press, 1981), 390.

senting her as one who "typifies and represents her sex" in her "religious sentiment." Thus, while Rossetti's choice of religious subjects is well within the feminine sphere, and again aligns her with Hemans, who by the end of her career was turning more to religious verse, Rossetti's use of biblical idiom begins to widen that sphere.

The distinction I am making here can perhaps be seen more clearly by comparing Hemans' poem "The Wings of the Dove" with Rossetti's "Sonnet from the Psalms" (1847). Both poets borrow from Ps. 55, in which David complains to the Lord: "Fearfulness and trembling are come upon me, and horror hath overwhelmed me. And I said, Oh that I had wings like a dove! for then would I fly away, and be at rest" (Ps. 55:5–6). Hemans begins with a clear echo of verse 6: "Oh! for thy wings, thou dove! / That I too might flee away, and be at rest." However, by the end of the poem, the speaker rejects David's complaint and expresses a willingness to return to woman's lot, with all its tears:

> For even by all the fears
> And thoughts that haunt my dreams—untold, unknown
>     And burning woman's tears,
> Pour'd from my eyes in silence and alone;
>
> *Had* I thy wings, thou dove!
> High 'midst the gorgeous isles of cloud to soar,
>     Soon the strong cords of love
> Would draw me earthwards—homewards—yet once more.[9]

Rossetti's "Sonnet from the Psalms," as the title suggests, weaves together the texts of several psalms (see Pss. 6, 39, 55). After imitating the psalmist's desire for the wings of the dove, Rossetti, unlike Hemans, includes no mention of a returning "earthwards" to home:

> All thro' the livelong night I lay awake
>     Watering my couch with tears of heaviness.
>     None stood beside me in my sore distress;—

---

9. Felicia Hemans, "The Wings of the Dove," *The Complete Works of Mrs. Hemans*, ed. Harriet Mary Browne Owen, 2 vols. (New York: D. Appleton, 1852), 1:578.

Then cried I to my heart: If thou wilt, break,
But be thou still; no moaning will I make,
    Nor ask man's help, nor kneel that he may bless.
So I kept silence in my haughtiness,
Till lo! the fire was kindled, and I spake
Saying: Oh that I had wings like to a dove,
    Then would I flee away and be at rest:
I would not pray for friends, or hope, or love,
    But still the weary throbbing of my breast;
And, gazing on the changeless heavens above,
    Witness that such a quietness is best.

(CP, 3:145)

The speaker rejects all earthly ties of affection, the very center of the feminine sphere; and the "tears of heaviness" with which the sonnet begins are replaced by "quietness," a word that again echoes Ecclesiastes: "Better is an handful with quietness than both the hands full with travail and vexation of spirit" (Eccles. 4:6). Furthermore, while Hemans' speaker reveals that she is a woman, the sex of Rossetti's speaker remains unidentified. However, again as with her other religious poems, her mingling of biblical texts and intonations associates her speaker with Old Testament voices, ones that are associated more with traditional definitions of masculinity than femininity.

One might also compare Rossetti's "Paradise" with Hemans' "The Better Land," a poem Rossetti most certainly read. (In 1844, William Michael gave his sister his copy of *The Sacred Harp*, an anthology of religious verse containing "The Better Land" and four other poems by Hemans.) Hemans only briefly employs the idiom of the Bible, and again her use of such language is feminized, so to speak, by her depiction of a mother answering her son's questions about heaven: "Eye hath not seen it, my gentle boy! / Ear hath not heard its deep songs of joy."[10] In Rossetti's "Paradise," on the other hand, the gender of the speaker is not specified. Furthermore, the speaker is not comforting a child but is telling of an actual dream of paradise and hope of seeing the reality itself:

10. Ibid., 2:262.

I hope to see these things again,
But not as once in dreams by night;
To see them with my very sight.

(CP, 1:222)

Finally, the poem concludes with an expression of hope that conveys an image of the speaker and, by implication, the woman poet as having a role in paradise: "[I hope] To have my part with all the saints, / And with my God" (1:222).

I am not arguing that Rossetti adopted the voice of the preacher, psalmist, and prophet merely to employ a voice of power the patriarchal society denied the woman poet. Certainly, she was not acquiring what William Michael Rossetti described as "truly minute and ready" knowledge of the Bible, merely to use the biblical idiom to empower her own poetic voice.[11] Rather, I am suggesting that her religious faith and the reading and thoughtful study of the Bible, which was an expression of that faith, played a central role in her response to the voices of her literary foremothers, specifically to the voice of the mournful woman who sees life in terms of earthly ties and affections, as so many of Hemans' speakers do, even those who speak of the "better land."

That Rossetti's religious experience played a very significant role in her response to the early nineteenth-century feminine poetic voice can be seen quite clearly when we consider her response to the voice of Letitia Elizabeth Landon. Whereas Hemans was seen as the poetess of home and a model of the "true woman," Landon's verse was seen as the model of feminine melancholy, that is, a melancholy caused by lost love: "No writer certainly has written more of Love and Sorrow than Mrs. Maclean [Landon]. She touches scarcely any other strings."[12] In her preface to *The Venetian Bracelet*, Landon herself described her subjects as "grief, disappointment, the fallen leaf, the faded flower, the broken heart, and the early grave." Rossetti's most recent biographer, Jan Marsh, indicates that when an adolescent Rossetti "devoured" this melancholy poetry.[13] Al-

11. William Michael Rossetti, ed., *The Poetical Works of Christina Georgina Rossetti* (London: Macmillan, 1904), lxix.

12. Rowton, *The Female Poets*, 425. See also Glennis Stephenson, *Letitia Landon: The Woman Behind L.E.L.* (Manchester: Manchester University Press, 1995).

13. Jan Marsh, *Christina Rossetti: A Writer's Life* (London: Jonathan Cape, 1994), 246.

though Rossetti's response to Hemans is rather indirect, more a question of shifting the feminine perspective from romance to religion and from home to heaven, her response to Landon is more direct and immediate. In other words, at times Rossetti actually appears to be echoing the world-weary voice of L.E.L. so as to critique its earth-bound perspective.

The following poem, simply entitled "Song," provides a characteristic example of Landon's mournful voice:

Oh never another dream can be
    Like that early dream of ours,
When the fairy Hope lay down to sleep,
    Like a child among the flowers.

But Hope has waken'd since, and wept,
    Like a rainbow, itself away;
And the flowers have faded and fallen around—
    We have none for a wreath to-day.

Now Wisdom wakes in the place of Hope,
    And our hearts are like winter hours:
Ah! after-life has been little worth
    That early dream of ours.[14]

Rossetti's well-known "Song" (1849) employs a similar imagery of faded flowers to embody a similar theme of loss:

Oh roses for the flush of youth,
    And laurel for the perfect prime;
But pluck an ivy branch for me
    Grown old before my time.

Oh violets for the grave of youth,
    And bay for those dead in their prime;

---

14. Letitia Elizabeth Landon, *The Poetical Works of Letitia Elizabeth Landon*, ed. F. S. Sypher (Delmar, N.Y.: Scholar's Facsimiles and Reprints, 1990), 329.

Give me the withered leaves I chose
Before in the old time.

(CP, 1:40)

The tone of this song, however, differs from that of Landon's. In Landon's poem is expressed a dominant note of regret; clearly, the speaker mourns lost hopes and still longs for the "early dream" of youth. In contrast, Rossetti's speaker, "grown old before [her] time," implies she never had that "early dream," and that she wants no pity, for she "chose" the "withered leaves."

The exact nature of this choice is unclear, but it can be clarified by considering the language of flowers, popular in the Victorian period and a language Rossetti often employed.[15] In assigning roses to youth, the speaker gives away love; in associating laurel with the prime of life, she rejects glory. In asking for ivy, a plant associated with fidelity because it is always green, she suggests that she has been faithful to this renunciation of earthly desires. Even on her grave she wants, not violets, a sign of humility, or bay, a sign of honor, especially for the poet, but the memorial of withered leaves. Such leaves are, of course, not part of the language of flowers but within the context of this poem can be read as a symbol of the speaker's renunciation of love and fame, the choice she made in the "old time." Whereas Landon's speaker still longs for earthly rewards, Rossetti's speaker willingly turns away. Behind Rossetti's poem lies a very different set of values and beliefs than that which underlies Landon's mournful song.

Such a difference can be further explored by comparing one of Landon's characteristic songs of death and farewell with what has become one of Rossetti's most famous songs of parting. In Landon's Vow of the Peacock, another distressed lady sings a song of farewell, claiming "her heart's best prayers" are all for the beloved who knows little of her passion:

Farewell! farewell! I would not leave
A single trace behind;

---

15. For an excellent discussion of Rossetti's use of Victorian flower lore, see Gisela Honnighausen, "Emblematic Tendencies in the Works of Christina Rossetti," Victorian Poetry 10 (spring 1972): 1–15.

Why should a thought, if me to grieve,
  Be left upon thy mind?
I would not have thy memory dwell
  Upon one thought of pain;
And sad it must be the farewell
  Of one who loved in vain.

However, while saying she does not want his memory to dwell upon her, the speaker undercuts that message with the last stanza, which serves to evoke guilt by contrasting her state with his: "Thy course is in the sun . . . For me,—my race is nearly run, / And its goal is the grave."[16] Rossetti's "Song" (1848) also bids farewell to the beloved by evoking images of the grave and might easily be likened to the mournful poetic voice of Landon:

When I am dead, my dearest,
  Sing no sad songs for me;
Plant thou no roses at my head,
  Nor shady cypress tree:
Be the green grass above me
  With showers and dewdrops wet;
And if thou wilt, remember,
  And if thou wilt, forget.

                                                                    (*CP*, 1:58)

However, a careful reading of these lines indicates that the speaker is actually rejecting the image of the grave, for that is not her "goal"; rather, it is some world of twilight dreaming:

I shall not see the shadows,
  I shall not feel the rain;
I shall not hear the nightingale
  Sing on, as if in pain:

16. The full text of *The Vow of the Peacock* is not included in the 1990 reprint of *Poetical Works* (1873); therefore, I have used *The Poetical Works of Miss Landon* (Philadelphia: E. L. Carey and H. Hart, 1838), 207.

And dreaming through the twilight
   That doth not rise nor set,
Haply I may remember,
   And haply may forget.

(1:58)

There is a playful, even lighthearted quality to the lines that counters the forlorn tones of Landon's broken-hearted woman. Also, it is important to notice that even though Landon's speaker is identified within *Vow of the Peacock* as female, Rossetti's speaker could be either male or female. Scholarship has consistently interpreted the voice as that of a woman, but actually there is no definite sign of gender in the poem. Moreover, Landon's speaker is still very much focused on earthly love and romance, whereas Rossetti's speaker has turned her attention to another world entirely, one of twilight dreaming, a world and a time that can be more thoroughly understood in terms of Rossetti's religious faith.

Throughout her life, Rossetti accepted the doctrine that after death the soul did not enter into its full heavenly reward but had to wait until the Second Coming of Christ, when all would be judged, the living and the dead, and those chosen would then enter into the New Jerusalem. As John Waller has noted in a very significant article on Rossetti, in the Advent season of December 1848 (Rossetti composed "When I am dead my dearest" during that month), Rossetti most likely heard several sermons delivered by the vicar of Christ Church, William Dodsworth, on the end of the world and the Second Coming.[17] Such sermons might easily have encouraged Rossetti to wonder about the time between death and resurrection.

Moreover, beginning in the 1840s and continuing throughout the century, considerable debate occurred within the church over the nature of the waiting time after death. The whole subject of eschatology—death, judgment, heaven, and hell—was, as Michael Wheeler points out, a "highly controversial subject in the Victorian age discussed not only in

17. John O. Waller, "Christ's Second Coming: Christina Rossetti and the Premillennialist William Dodsworth," *Bulletin of the New York Public Library* 73 (September 1969): 465–82. See also Linda E. Marshall, "What the Dead Are Doing Underground: Hades and Heaven in the Writings of Christina Rossetti," *Victorian Newsletter* 72 (fall 1987): 55–60.

sermons but in general periodicals as well.[18] Indeed, such subjects were possibly topics of discussion within Rossetti's immediate family, especially among the women of her family, who were devout churchgoers. Significantly, at the time of Rossetti's death, her library contained an 1831 copy of John Peers's *The Scripture Doctrine of the State of the Departed Both Before and After the Resurrection,* which was once owned by her maternal grandmother. In this small book, Peers discusses at length the soul's experiences in the "intermediate state," that is, the state between death and resurrection, concluding that this waiting time, though one of "rest," must also be a time of "enjoyment" and not "mere cessation from labour."[19] This state of "rest" may well be akin to Rossetti's world of twilight dreaming, a world that was not at all the static world of rest one unfamiliar with Rossetti's faith might imagine. Indeed, John Henry Newman, a theologian Rossetti much admired even after he became a Roman Catholic, stresses in his sermon on the subject that the spiritual state after death and before the resurrection is not a time of stasis, for it is "full of excellent visions and wonderful revelations."[20]

Rossetti's transcendent view of life, which focused as much on the future as the present, should be considered when assessing her response to the feminine poetic tradition represented by both Hemans and Landon, for such an eschatological perspective clearly plays a major role in her assessment of the woman poet's voice. Although Rossetti was born into a society that expected her to write of love, and the sorrow caused by love, because she was a woman, she was also living at a time when religious debates were an important part of her immediate environment, debates not about woman's heart but about the human soul. In a sense, the warn-

18. Michael Wheeler, *Death and the Future Life in Victorian Literature and Theology* (Cambridge: Cambridge University Press, 1990), xii. See also Geoffrey Rowell, *Hell and the Victorians: A Study of the Nineteenth-Century Theological Controversies Concerning Eternal Punishment and the Future Life* (Oxford: Clarendon Press, 1974).

19. John Peers, *The Scripture Doctrine of the State of the Departed Both Before and After the Resurrection* (London: Hatchard and Son, 1831), 18. For evidence that this book was familiar to Rossetti, see *List of Books Being Relics of the Rossetti Family Purchased from the Executor of the Late Christina G. Rossetti and Now Being Offered for Sale by J. M. Tregaskis,* no. 341 (1896).

20. John Henry Newman, "The Intermediate State," *Parochial and Plain Sermons* (London: Rivingtons, 1870), 3:374.

ings of Rossetti's faith regarding the soul were heard more loudly than the warnings of her culture regarding women poets' proper sphere. Her preoccupation with spiritual issues of damnation and redemption may well have diminished any pressure she might have felt to write strictly "female poetry," that is, poetry in which the voice of the weeping woman, a woman still focused on the sorrow of this world, establishes the dominant tone.

That Rossetti's response to Landon was shaped by her interest in eschatology can be seen most clearly in *Maude*, a novella in prose and verse that Rossetti wrote sometime in 1849–1850. *Maude* has often been read autobiographically. The heroine's age, state of health and mind, and, especially, the fact she is a poet have led critics to see Maude as a version of Rossetti during her adolescent years. Certainly, the similarities between Maude and Rossetti do invite an autobiographical reading. However, *Maude* is not a diary entry or a confessional piece but a crafted story.[21] Thus, even though the novella has autobiographical echoes, more attention should be given to ways in which this story is not just a private reflection, revealing Rossetti's inner world, but a public comment. Indeed, *Maude* can be read as Rossetti's attempt at a public response to the feminine melancholy strain of poetry she inherits from her foremothers, especially Landon.

Rossetti did not publish *Maude*, but the finished state of the manuscript suggests she wrote with an audience in mind, and this audience seems to have been primarily female, for the plot involves young Victorian women and the choices life offers them: marriage, the convent, or perhaps the career of a poet of melancholy verse.[22] Mary represents the choice of marriage and seems quite happy in that choice; Magdalen chooses the convent and again is portrayed as content. In contrast, Maude, the poet, struggles with the options offered. She is described by the narrator as "dissatisfied with her circumstances, her friends and herself" (*M*, 49). At times, Rossetti uses Maude's poetry as a device to reveal

21. For a recent and insightful analysis of *Maude* that does draw attention to its literary qualities, see Sharon Smulders, *Christina Rossetti Revisited* (New York: Twayne, 1996), 23–32.

22. Rossetti's manuscript of *Maude: Prose and Verse* is held at the Huntington Library, San Marino, California. It has the appearance of a fair copy prepared for publication. I would like to thank David A. Kent for this information.

her heroine's dissatisfaction, and the poetry Maude writes often resembles Landon's weary melancholy strain.

The first poem included is the sonnet that begins, "Yes, I too could face death and never shrink," which Maude appears to write in a spontaneous manner reminiscent of Landon's poet-speakers. Although the speaker asserts her "courage" in claiming that she is willing to face suffering and not commit suicide, nevertheless she appears to long for the grave and to be rather proud of the extent of her suffering: "Thousands taste the full cup; who drains the lees?—" (*M*, 30). That Rossetti wants the reader to see Maude as affected and perhaps indulging in dramatic posturing is suggested by the narrative comment that follows immediately after the last line of the poem: "having done which [having written the sonnet] she yawned, leaned back in her chair, and wondered how she should fill up the time till dinner" (30). At this stage in the story, Maude's suffering appears self-indulgent and exaggerated. As readers, we see that she has a loving mother, friends who care for her, and a poetic talent recognized at least by her immediate circle.

As the story progresses, however, the reader discovers that there is some cause for distress in that Maude accuses herself of hypocrisy. She attends church and yet, as her sonnet beginning "I listen to the holy antheming" reveals, "vanity enters" with her, and her "love / Soars not to Heaven, but grovelleth below" (*M*, 51). Thus, unlike a Landon heroine, who suffers because of ill-fated love, Maude suffers because she feels guilty; her melancholy is religious, not romantic. In an important conversation with Agnes, her calm and well-adjusted cousin who serves as her foil, she states that she feels unable to receive Holy Communion. In his preface to the first published version of the novella, William Michael Rossetti seemed to realize that Maude's refusal to receive Holy Communion was significant, but he nevertheless concluded that "so far as my own views of right and wrong go, I cannot see that the much-reprehended Maude commits a single serious fault from title-page to finis" (reproduced in *M*, 80). Yet one should remember he was not in sympathy with his sister's faith. Rossetti certainly intends the reader to see Maude's refusal to receive Communion as serious, for Agnes' response indicates that Maude's behavior could lead to endangering her soul: "Stop; you cannot mean, —you do not know what you are saying. You will go no more? Only think, if the struggle is so hard now, what it will be when you reject all help" (52). Agnes continues to try to persuade Maude to receive Communion by speaking of her own spiritual struggles: "I was once on the very point of acting as you propose. I was perfectly wretched: harassed and discouraged on all sides. But then it struck me—you won't be angry?—that it was so ungrateful to follow my own fancies, instead of at least endeavouring to do God's Will: and so foolish too; for if our safety is not in obedience, where is it?" (52). Agnes realizes that in terms of religious doctrine, Maude's refusal to receive the Eucharist places her soul in danger, for as the catechism states in the Book of Common Prayer, both baptism and the "Supper of the Lord" are "necessary to salvation." That Agnes fears that Maude may well lose her soul is suggested by her pleading, "It is not too late: besides think for one moment what will be the end of this. We must all die; what if you keep to your resolution and do as you have said, and receive the Blessed Sacrament no more?" (53).

Maude's vanity has resulted in much more than pride in her poetic talent. Through Agnes, Rossetti makes it clear that Maude's rejection of the Eucharist is a rejection of Christ as her savior, and that therefore she must turn back to Christ if she is to be saved. After this scene with Agnes, a Christmas carol is heard outside Maude's window reinforcing Agnes' message: "He is our Messenger; beside, / He is our Door, and Path, and Guide" (*M,* 56). This is a carol Rossetti herself wrote, and her insertion of it at this point in the story can be read as Rossetti's response to her troubled heroine. Although Maude hears this carol at this moment, she remains "unpenitent." However, this is the lowest point in her religious crisis, and after this night she does begin to return to her faith. First, we are told she does receive Communion. Furthermore, the poems written before her death indicate a significant change of heart.

Rossetti does resort to the device of a convenient accident leading to Maude's death as a way of bringing closure to the story but does not end the story with a death scene. Rather, she concludes with a description of Agnes choosing to keep three of Maude's poems. That Rossetti leaves the well-adjusted Agnes in charge of Maude's poetry is significant and has been too often overlooked in autobiographical readings of this story. Moreover, when Agnes' selection of poems is read in the order of the supposed dates of composition, the series of three poems suggests that Maude did find spiritual peace before she died.

In this arrangement, which serves to conclude Maude's life story, Rossetti continues to answer and revise the weeping voice of Landon's poetic heroines. "Sleep let me sleep, for I am sick of care" is dated ten days after Maude's accident, and it is the most reminiscent of Landon:

> Shut out the light; thicken the heavy air
> With drowsy incense; let a distant stream
> Of music lull me, languid as a dream,
> Soft as the whisper of a Summer sea.
> . . . . . . . . . . . . . . .
> But bring me poppies brimmed with sleepy death,
> And ivy choking what it garlandeth.
>
> (*M,* 72)

In these lines one hears echoes of Landon's heroines who desire the forgetfulness of death, and even though Rossetti's poem ends with some hint of rebirth in the image of "quickened dust," the graveyard image so characteristic of Landon's work dominates this lament. Nevertheless, the second poem, "evidently composed at a subsequent period" (73), indicates a changed perspective. Although the speaker calls death to come quickly, it is not to bring an end to life and its pain, but to hasten the new life that must follow:

> Birth follows hard on death,
>     Life on withering:
> Hasten, we shall come the sooner
>     Back to pleasant Spring.
>
> (*M,* 73)

In this poem, the worries and complaints of the individual voice are gone. Furthermore, there is no suggestion that the speaker does not expect to see the return of spring.

The last poem is especially significant, for it is in this sonnet that we hear the poetic voice of biblical authority, so characteristic of Rossetti but not of either Hemans or Landon. "What is it Jesus saith unto the soul?—" is "dated the morning before [Maude's] death," and thus Rossetti encourages the reader to see the sonnet as representing the last stage in her heroine's earthly struggle. The answer given to the opening lines quotes Jesus' message to his disciples: "Take up the Cross, and come and follow me." Again, as with the first two poems in this series, there is the theme of pain and suffering, but now such pain is placed firmly in a Christian context: "no man may be / Without the Cross, wishing to win the goal" (*M,* 75). The acceptance of suffering is seen as necessary for salvation, yet hope is offered. Those that suffer will be able to bear the trial, for Christ will be there: "He will control the powers of darkness." Moreover, at the end of time, he will release the soul from all suffering and waiting. Then he shall come again to call the faithful soul home:

> He will be with thee, helping, strengthening,
> Until it is enough: for lo, the day
> Cometh when He shall call thee: thou shalt hear
> His Voice That says: "Winter is past, and Spring
> Is come; arise, My Love, and come away."—

(M, 75)

Rossetti's speaker is not lamenting her predicament but comforting the reader by foretelling the Second Coming of Christ. Again, Rossetti's use of the biblical allusion is significant. In the last lines Rossetti's speaker not only echoes the Song of Songs (2:10–11), but she does so in terms of Christian eschatology. The words of the bridegroom calling his beloved to join with him in a springtime of love are to be read as Christ calling the soul to awake and join him in heaven. Thus, *spring,* a word read in the first of these three poems as a mere season associated with youth and gaiety, by the third poem is to be read as symbolic of the resurrection of the body and the final entrance into heaven. In these three poems, Rossetti borrows from Landon but does so ultimately in order to answer her foremother's melancholy lament with tales of rebirth and with echoes of the Song of Songs. Maude, who begins the story echoing one of Landon's weary women, has died thinking not of the forgetfulness of the grave but of the Second Coming of Christ.

That the young Rossetti read Landon in this way, that is, as a poet singing mournfully of lost love without much hope of awakening to a larger spiritual love, is further suggested by her renaming the poem she first entitled "Spring" (written in February 1859) as "L.E.L.," the signature Landon most often used when publishing her poems. The poem begins with a speaker, presumably L.E.L., telling that her "heart is breaking for a little love" and therefore she can "feel no spring" even though the season has begun, a characteristic claim of one of Landon's speakers. Indeed, the first four stanzas can be read as depicting a typical Landon mournful woman. However, in stanza five, the speaker wonders if the "saints" and "angels guess the truth." This thought is characteristic of so many of Rossetti's speakers, who look forward to last things more than any of Landon's comparatively earthbound speakers. Rossetti's speaker then quotes saint and angel:

> Yet saith a saint: "Take patience for thy scathe;"
>      Yet saith an angel: "Wait, for thou shalt prove
> True best is last, true life is born of death,
>      O thou, heart-broken for a little love.
>           Then love shall fill thy girth,
>           And love make fat thy dearth,
> When new spring builds new heaven and clean new earth."
>
> (CP, 1:154–55)

This stanza echoes multiple biblical texts. The most significant, however, is the allusion to Rev. 21:1 ("And I saw a new heaven and a new earth"), for this last line makes clear that the "spring" Rossetti is referring to is that which is to follow Christ's Second Coming, when, in the language of the Song of Songs, the bridegroom would come to call his beloved home.

Rossetti's early poetry, written during the 1840s and 1850s, certainly has mournful strains of what might be considered distinctly feminine suffering, poetic strains that link her to Hemans and Landon. However, there is ample evidence in these poems and her novella *Maude* that she wants to define for herself a place where she, a woman poet, can speak as preacher and prophet of the vanity of this world and the need to prepare for the next by waiting and watching for the Second Coming.

One might conclude that this transcendent vision would mean that Rossetti's poetry is removed from any sociohistorical context; in fact, such a view dominated assessments of Rossetti's poetry for much of this century. She was said not to belong to the Victorian age but rather to the seventeenth century or even to some vague medieval time. On the contrary, as I have indicated above, her preoccupation with eschatology was characteristic of many Victorians who still believed in God. Furthermore, Rossetti's transcendent view actually involved her in very specific nineteenth-century concerns relevant to Victorian women, such as the revival of Anglican religious sisterhoods.

*two*

# ROSSETTI AND THE
# CONVENT QUESTION

✝

AS A YOUNG WOMAN, ROSSETTI WAS INFLUENCED BY THE OX-
ford Movement, or tractarianism, as it is also called, which sought to revi-
talize the spiritual life of the Church of England and had about it a strong
ascetic element. Indeed, one recent historian sees the Oxford Movement
"primarily as a spiritual force, a quest for holiness through self-denial and
mortification of bodily and worldly appetites." Rossetti's introduction to
the views and aims of this movement was through her parish church. By
1844 she was, along with her mother and sister, attending Christ Church,
Albany Street, whose incumbent minister, William Dodsworth, was an
admirer and follower of Edward Pusey, a leading figure of the movement
who sometimes preached there. Furthermore, the first Anglican religious
sisterhood, the Community of the Holy Cross, formed under Pusey's
guidance, was established at Park Village West, within the parish of
Christ Church. It was founded during the Easter season of 1845, and for
seven years, until the order moved to Osnaburgh Street, Christ Church
was its "spiritual home."[1]

---

1. Peter Benedict Nockles, *The Oxford Movement in Context: Anglican High Churchmanship, 1760–1857* (Cambridge: Cambridge University Press, 1994), 184; Thomas Jay Wil-
liams and Allen Walter Campbell, *The Park Village Sisterhood* (London: Society for Promoting Christian Knowledge, 1965), 21.

The figure of Magdalen in *Maude* is most likely based on this sister-hood, and the description of Magdalen as "calm and happy" suggests that the young Rossetti was an early supporter of the conventual revival. Furthermore, this seeming initial acceptance of both the sisterhoods and the ascetic impulse they embody became open support in 1860, when her sister Maria, a woman Rossetti not only loved but also greatly admired, joined the Society of All Saints as an outer sister, becoming fully professed in 1875. For many years, Rossetti was closely associated with this order, staying at the All Saints' convalescent home when Maria was ill, supporting the community's charitable efforts, and apparently arranging with her brother William Michael to leave the sisterhood a financial gift after their deaths. Rossetti records in his personal reminiscences that just before his sister died, she indicated that she was leaving him two thousand pounds, on the understanding that he would bequeath this money to religious organizations.[2] After his death, All Saints did indeed receive one thousand pounds.

William Michael suggested in a letter to Rossetti's first biographer, Mackenzie Bell, that she might have actually been at some point an outer sister of All Saints: "She was (I rather think) an outer sister—but in no sort of way professed—of the Convent which Maria afterwards joined."[3] According to the earliest records available in the archives of All Saints, outer sisters were "ladies who desire[d] to be joined to the third Order of a Religious Community, with the view either of preparing for a religious, or of sanctifying a secular vocation," and who, once received into the order in such a capacity, were to "partake in the prayers and works of the Community" and "to subject themselves to a Rule of Life."[4] Some scholars have read William Michael's letter to Bell as proof that Rossetti did indeed become such an outer sister; however, her name does not appear in the records of All Saints in that capacity. (Women who became outer sisters were actually "received" into the order during a religious service designed for that purpose, and records were kept of such

2. William Michael Rossetti, *Some Reminiscences,* 2 vols. (1906; rpr., New York: AMS Press, 1970), 2:535.

3. Mackenzie Bell, *Christina Rossetti* (Boston: Roberts Brothers, 1898), 60.

4. *Rule for the Outer Sisters of All Saints,* before 1893. I would like to thank the sisters of All Saints, and especially Sister Margaret, for allowing me to examine the archives.

services.) Furthermore, a letter from Rossetti to her friend Caroline Gemmer makes it clear that she never seriously considered following the path Maria took: "So you think I once trembled on the 'convent threshold'—Not seriously ever, tho' I went through a sort of romantic impression on the subject like many young people. No, I feel no drawing in that direction: really, of the two, I might perhaps have less unadaptedness in some ways to the hermit life. But I suppose the niche really suited to me is the humble family nook I occupy, nor am I hankering after a loftier."[5]

Although such evidence indicates that Rossetti never sought any formal commitment to a religious life, she periodically turned throughout her career as a writer to the conventual life for subject matter. Several of her poems focus on the life of a nun or novice: "The Novice" (1847), "Three Nuns" (1849–1850), "The Convent Threshold" (1858), "'The Master is Come, and Calleth for Thee'" (before 1875), "An 'Immurata' Sister" (before 1881), and "Soeur Louise de la Misericorde (1674)" (before 1881). Considering these poems within the context of the movement to establish Anglican sisterhoods not only adds to our understanding of Rossetti's attitude toward a woman's place in Victorian society but also enlarges our understanding of a major theme characterizing her poetry, that of renunciation.

Anglican religious sisterhoods did not meet with easy acceptance.[6] Throughout Rossetti's life, the convent question, as it was called, was a subject of intense debate, and a debate not limited to the Church of England hierarchy. The Victorian community as a whole debated the merits and dangers of allowing women to enter into the religious life. Articles on the subject appeared not only in Protestant religious periodicals such as *Good Words* and *The Congregationalist* but also in more general periodicals such as *Macmillan's*, *Fraser's*, and even *Punch*.[7] Newspapers also cov-

5. Quoted in Antony H. Harrison, *Christina Rossetti in Context* (Chapel Hill: University of North Carolina Press, 1988), 189.

6. For a thorough discussion of Anglican sisterhoods, see Michael Hill, *The Religious Order* (London: Heinemann, 1973).

7. See J. M. Ludlow, "Sisterhoods," *Good Words* 4 (1864): 493–502; "Sisterhoods in the Anglican Church," *Congregationalist* 7 (1878): 310–13; "Convent of the Belgravians," *Punch,* October 19, 1850, 163; "The Pilgrims to Rome," *Punch,* May 31, 1851, 230–31; "Two Views of the Convent Question, *Macmillan's Magazine* 19 (1869): 434–43; and "Sisters and Sisterhoods," *Fraser's Magazine* 84 (1871): 638–49.

ered the issue. At one point, the *Times* reported on a group of opponents who were calling for the government to inspect these newly established religious houses, claiming that women were being held in Anglican convents against their will.[8] (Such claims were apparently groundless but not uncommon.) Among nineteenth-century novels during these years, signs of sentiment clearly opposed to establishing Anglican sisterhoods can also be found. Charles Kingsley's *Yeast: A Problem* (1848), Harriet Martineau's short novel *Sister Anna's Probation* (1861–62), and the relatively unknown E. Jane Whately's *Maude; or the Anglican Sister of Mercy* (1869), all question the value, and at times the morality, of the convent life. According to Robert Wolff, the death-in-life figure of Miss Havisham in *Great Expectations* can be seen as reflecting Dickens' "apprehension" about convents. Finally, even the people in the street at times showed disapproval at the sight of an Anglican nun. In her memoirs, Mother Caroline Mary, the second mother superior of All Saints Convent, notes, "When at length I received 'the habit' I remember as we [she and her fellow nuns] walked in the street passers by often scoffed or showed positive hatred of our outward dress, made faces at us and called us 'sisters of misery' and one's own relations even pitied us."[9]

Much of this disapproval was related to a general suspicion of Roman Catholicism that was still very much a part of British culture at the time. Any practice perceived as mirroring this faith was often seen by many as a dangerous sign of popery. A petition sent to Queen Victoria from the "Ladies of Bath," with more than two thousand signatures, indicating their opposition to Anglican sisterhoods concludes, "If they [Anglican sisterhoods] are not insidious attempts to increase the influence of the Papacy, they do generate principles which prepare minds for the reception of the doctrines of Rome, which are, and always have been, injurious to the best interests of your Majesty's crown and realm."[10] Those opposed

---

8. Parliamentary debates on the inspection of religious houses occurred in the early 1850s. For coverage of these debates, see the *Guardian*, June 8, 1853, and the *Times*, March 15, 1851.

9. Robert Lee Wolff, *Gains and Losses: Novels of Faith and Doubt in Victorian England* (New York: Garland, 1977), 3–4; Memoirs of Sister Caroline Mary, ms, All Saints Archives, Oxford.

10. A copy of this petition can be found in M. Hobart Seymour, *Convents or Nunneries: A Lecture* (London: Seeleys, 1852), 60.

to sisterhoods often sought to win support for their position by portraying Roman Catholicism as an oppressive religion leading to unmentionable horrors. For example, Rev. M. Hobbart Seymour, whose lecture on convents led to the Bath petition, describes the Catholic nunneries of Spain and Italy, which he calls "prisons," as places "where every vice of earth and every crime of hell is perpetrated, and where the shrieks of outraged innocence, and the death-sighs of a broken heart, are suppressed and stifled within the walls, and never can be heard in the outer world."[11]

However, if one looks beyond the inflammatory language sometimes used by those opposed to the conventual life, one finds that it is not so much Roman Catholicism that is feared but the vow of celibacy.[12] Rev. Seymour, for example, writes at length about a young woman's "flower and blossom" being sacrificed to such an "unnatural" vow.[13] Seymour clearly implies that the natural choice for a woman is marriage. As social historians have made clear, most Victorians considered marriage a woman's highest goal and noblest vocation, and thus a vow of celibacy was seen as a direct attack on the Victorian celebration of marriage, motherhood, and family. Many Victorians simply found it impossible to believe that a woman would willingly choose to renounce the possibility of a life as a wife and mother for the life of the nun. Some of those who did support Anglican convents spoke of them only as a way of dealing with "superfluous" women. A woman should consider becoming a nun only if she had not found a husband—it was "a salvage operation."[14]

Given such views, it is not surprising, therefore, that all the early Anglican orders were active, not contemplative. There was little support for the idea that a woman might choose to remove herself from family and society to devote herself to meditation and prayer. Although some of the early supporters of Anglican sisterhoods, such as John Henry Newman,

11. Ibid., 22.
12. For detailed discussions of the debate on allowing vows within Anglican sisterhoods, see A. M. Allchin, *The Silent Rebellion: Anglican Religious Communities* (London: SCM Press, 1958), 161–68; and Hill, *The Religious Order*, 243–48.
13. Seymour, *Convents or Nunneries*, 57, 17.
14. John Shelton Reed, "A Female Movement: The Feminization of Nineteenth-Century Anglo-Catholicism," *Historical Magazine of the Protestant Episcopal Church* 77 (1988): 229. See also Martha Vicinus, *Independent Women: Work and Community for Single Women, 1850–1920* (Chicago: University of Chicago Press, 1985).

Edward Pusey, and Priscilla Sellon, may have strongly favored reinstituting sisterhoods for the sake of the consecrated life, the majority of supporters appear to have favored Anglican sisterhoods as a means of solving social problems and, more important, problems that were also seen as within woman's sphere of influence: "Who can better undertake the charge of hospitals, homes for unmarried females in our great cities, houses for orphans, institutions for sending out nurses, or for educating the blind and the deaf and dumb than Sisters of Mercy,—gentle, tender, collected, trained to these various works?" For these supporters, establishing organized religious sisterhoods was a way to extend the feminine sphere beyond home to the larger community. Thus, even though a woman who became an Anglican nun moved beyond the immediate sphere of the Victorian home, she nevertheless could still be viewed as a nurturing, maternal figure, serving others. Even Anna Jameson, an advocate of women's rights and of Anglican sisterhoods, denounces contemplative orders as unhealthy: If women were allowed to form contemplative orders, "there would necessarily ensue, in lighter characters, frivolity, idleness, and sick disordered fancies; and in superior minds, ascetic pride, gloom and impatience."[15]

When we turn to Rossetti's convent poems, with this overview of the convent question in mind, we can see that she is setting herself in opposition to those who would claim marriage to be the only noble choice for a woman, and that she is even resisting such views as Jameson expresses. For Rossetti, to choose the consecrated religious life, even the contemplative life, was not foolish or unnatural, and certainly Rossetti did not imagine such a choice leading to "disordered fancies." Rather, becoming a nun represented a genuine choice a woman might make. Moreover, a woman who was called to such a vocation was to be revered, not pitied. Rossetti's convent poems indicate that while many of her contemporaries saw nuns as choosing a life-in-death existence, she saw them as wise virgins choosing life.

Significantly, in none of her convent poems, written over a span of approximately thirty years, does Rossetti employ imagery of imprison-

---

15. W. J. Butler, "A Short Preface on Sisterhoods," in *On Penitentiary Work* (Oxford: Parker, 1861), ix; Anna Jameson, *Sisters of Charity: At Home and Abroad* (London: Spottiswoode, 1855), 46.

ment or death when depicting convent life. Moreover, whereas those vehemently opposed to religious sisterhoods depict the convent as a place of vice, misery, and death, Rossetti's speakers more often see the world outside convent walls as one of misery and vice, and the convent as a refuge from such a place. At times, Rossetti's depiction of the convent world suggests that women are actually safer inside such walls. Even in Rossetti's first convent poem, "The Novice" (1847), written before her mature views were formed, the speaker describes the world she leaves behind as "full of all ill and fear-oppressed" (*CP*, 3:140). And the very first lines of "The Convent Threshold," Rossetti's most famous convent poem, associate this world with the violent imagery of blood:

There's blood between us, love, my love,
There's father's blood, there's brother's blood;
And blood's a bar I cannot pass:
I choose the stairs that mount above.

(*CP*, 1:61)

In "Soeur Louise de la Miséricorde (1674)," a poem based on the life of Louise de la Vallière, mistress to Louis XIV, who entered the Carmelite order after she lost the king's affection, Louise dwells on the destructive vanity of worldly life, which brought her not roses but thorns, and a memory of a "bottomless gulf of mire" (2:119–20). The speaker of "An 'Immurata' Sister" describes the world as "empty" and predicts it will "soon die" (2:120). Similarly, the third nun in Rossetti's "Three Nuns" sees the world she leaves behind as "waxing old" and imagines that some day its heart will be "dead and cold," while her heart will then "beat with a new life" (3:191).

Moreover, not only do Rossetti's speakers see this world of time as dying, but they can also imagine an eternal life beyond death. In four of the five poems employing the persona of the nun or novice, such immortality is spoken of as an absolute reality. (Only in Rossetti's "The Novice" is there no mention of heaven.) The "immurata" sister sees her soul as "mount[ing] higher and higher," a "whole burnt-offering" for God. The second nun in the poetic series "Three Nuns" believes that if she is saved, she shall "wake again," in heaven. The third nun in the series imagines that after death, "The City builded without hands / Shall safely shut [her] in," and even the first speaker, the one who exhibits the weakest signs of a genuine religious vocation, speaks of the "flush of Paradise" (*CP*, 3:190, 191, 188). In addition, although the speakers of "The Novice," "The Convent Threshold," and "Soeur Louise" appear to seek the convent motivated more by ill-fated love than by a desire for the religious life, in the two poems of Rossetti's mature work, "The Convent Threshold" and "Soeur Louise," both women speak of the spiritual life with certainty. Soeur Louise's regret over the vanity of earthly desire implies that there is a spiritual desire she should have experienced more strongly: "Oh vanity of vanities, desire; / Stunting my hope which might have strained up higher" (*CP*, 2:120). Although the speaker of "The Convent Threshold" is still very much in love with her earthly lover, she recognizes that such love did lead to sin: "You sinned with me a pleasant sin," and she urges him to "repent" so he might be with her in heaven (*CP*, 1:63). Repeatedly, Rossetti's convent poems convey the message that the invisible world of the spirit is indeed real, even for a woman whose heart is still earthbound.

The figure of the brokenhearted nun, that is, the woman seeking refuge in the convent only after disappointment in love, could be read as reinforcing the belief that no woman could possibly prefer the life of the nun to that of wife. The novice or nun as love's victim was a common figure used by poets and especially artists, during the first half of the nineteenth century, to convey just that message.[16] Certainly, Rossetti's convent poems of women unhappy in love can be linked to this literary figure; however, Rossetti's emphasis on the reality of the spiritual life sets them apart.

One can better see this distinctive difference by comparing Rossetti's treatment of the theme to that found in Landon's "Clematis" and "Louise, Duchess de la Vallière."[17] Although Landon's poems are published before the debate over Anglican convents becomes intense, they do represent the tradition against which Rossetti is writing.

16. For an excellent discussion of the image of the nun in Victorian art, see Susan P. Casteras, "Virgin Vows: The Early Victorian Artists' Portrayal of Nuns and Novices," *Victorian Studies* 24 (winter 1981): 157–84.

17. "Clematis" was included in Landon's annual *Flowers of Loveliness* (1838), and "Louise" was published in *Fisher's Drawing Room Scrapbook* (1839). I would like to thank Glennis Stephenson for kindly drawing my attention to these poems, and for providing me with information on the illustration accompanying "Clematis."

"Clematis" was written to accompany an illustration in which two nuns are standing by a cross entwined with clematis. Characteristic of Landon, this illustration appears to have inspired her to write of broken-hearted women. Flower lore indicates that among the many names given to clematis are "love," because of its "clinging habit," and "virgin's bower."[18] Perhaps Landon had both in mind when she wrote her poem. The speaker expresses some regret that the convent is now in ruins, but she does so only because she feels a quiet place is still needed for a "broken-hearted" woman with a "weary eye": "Still is the quiet cloister wanted, / For those who wear a weary eye . . . / Who have one only wish—to die." The poem concludes with the voice of some imagined nun longing not for heaven, and not even for a reunion with her lover in heaven, but only death: "There might the last prayer rise to heaven, / 'My God! I pray thee, let me die.'" Unlike Rossetti's "The Convent Threshold," there is no mention of a more glorious spiritual life to follow death.

Similarly, in Landon's "Louise, Duchess de la Vallière," the focus is again on lost love, not the spiritual life. Louise's thoughts are all for the king: "I only pray for him, / His coldness more than my own fault bewailing." In Landon's version of the duchess' story, King Louis is very much a figure of love, whereas in Rossetti's treatment of the same subject, he is not even mentioned. And unlike Rossetti's Soeur Louise, Landon's speaker achieves no clear recognition of the vanity of earthly desire. In both these poems, Landon employs the convent motif to stress the painfulness of romantic love from a woman's point of view, but unlike Rossetti, she does not show a woman attempting to renounce that love in order to see heaven.

When considering how Rossetti has employed the theme of romantic love in these two poems, it is important to note that each of these novices is also a fallen woman, that is, each is guilty of illicit sexual love. Louise was the king's mistress, and the speaker in "The Convent Threshold" suggests some sexual sin in her reference to the "pleasant sin" of which she and her "love" are both guilty. Rossetti's views on fallen women are complex and are discussed in more detail in Chapter 4; here, however, it

18. Charles M. Skinner, *Myths and Legends of Flowers, Trees, Fruits, and Plants* (London: Lippincott, 1911), 88.

is helpful to recall that according to William Michael Rossetti, his sister "supplemented" her reading of the Bible with St. Augustine's *Confessions* and Thomas à Kempis' *Imitation of Christ*.[19] Both these works warn against concupiscence, but especially the *Confessions*. Significantly, when Augustine tells of his conversion, he connects it to the precise moment when he read the following biblical text from Paul's letter to the Romans: "Let us walk honestly, as in the day; not in rioting and drunkenness, not in chambering and wantonness, not in strife and envying. But put ye on the Lord Jesus Christ, and make not provision for the flesh, to fulfil the lusts thereof" (Rom. 13:13–14). Although Rossetti's portrayal of sexual love in "The Convent Threshold" and "Soeur Louise" should not be seen as her final thoughts on the subject, that these women seek to follow the path of St. Augustine and St. Paul can be read as a definite sign of their spiritual progress.[20]

For Rossetti, the convent was not merely an escape from the sorrow and pain of this world but a place to see more clearly the spiritual life to come. Not surprisingly, therefore, the world of Rossetti's convent poems is more suggestive of the contemplative life than the active life of the Anglican Sisters of Mercy. Only once, and that is in her short story *Maude*, does she depict a nun engaged in a work of mercy. (Magdalen is seen walking with some poor children.) In her poetry, Rossetti does not depict nuns moving about in the world; the nuns of Rossetti's poems speak from within convent walls, where they are engaged not in works of mercy but in spiritual struggles. We see them pray, ask others to pray for them, plead with a lover to repent, question the value of romantic love, or long for heaven and the moment of seeing God face to face. For Rossetti, the nun is a woman who is looking forward beyond this life and beyond the end of time.

Significantly, in *Maude*, Sister Magdalen is viewed by the poet-heroine in just those terms. Once Maude knows that Sister Magdalen is interested in her poetry, she sends her a copy of a poem that foretells the end of time and warns of the judgment that will follow:

19. William Michael Rossetti, ed., *Poetical Works of Christina Georgina Rossetti* (London: Macmillan, 1904), lxix.

20. For a more detailed discussion of the influence of St. Augustine on Rossetti, see Harrison, *Christina Rossetti in Context*, 96–101, 138–41.

Let us see our lamps are lighted, duly
　　Fed with oil, nor wanting more:
Let us pray while yet the Lord will hear us,
　　For the time is almost o'er;
Yea, the end of all is very near us;
　　Yea, the Judge is at the door.
Let us pray now while we may;
　　It will be too late to pray
When the quick and dead shall all
　　Rise at the last trumpet call.

(CP, 3:175–76)

Rossetti emphasizes the appropriateness of this poem for the nun, and for what Maude refers to as "convent walls," by indicating that Magdalen learned this poem "by heart."

The reference to the need for lighted lamps alludes to the parable of the wise and foolish virgins (Matt. 25:1–13). This allusion carries with it a clear warning of damnation. Those foolish virgins who did not have oil for their lamps were not ready for the bridegroom and therefore were not invited into the marriage feast; in other words, those not ready for the Second Coming of Christ would not be admitted into the kingdom of heaven. Again, it is important to recall that Rossetti was among those Victorians who believed in hell and the possibility of eternal damnation. Certain poems, such as "The World" and "I Know You Not," suggest that belief, and her later devotional prose works make it explicit. In *The Face of the Deep*, for example, when speaking of the need to "watch" for Christ the Bridegroom, she writes: "Nor is it any trivial matter which depends on our watchfulness. According as we watch, or watch not, Christ will come to save or punish" (*FD*, 90). Although Rossetti believed in a merciful and loving God, her comments in *Time Flies* on "the bottomless pit," a phrase appearing often in the book of Revelation, indicate that because she accepted the doctrine of free will she believed it quite possible that a man or woman might indeed choose their own damnation:

But in the bottomless pit I see a symbol of that eternal antago-
nism and recession by which created free will seems able to defy

and baffle even the Almighty Will of the Creator. At a standstill, anywhere, though on the extreme boundary of time or space, the sinner might be overtaken by the pursuing Love of God: but once passing beyond those limits, eternity sets in; the everlasting attitude appears taken up, the everlasting recoil commenced. Beyond the grave no promise is held out to us of shipwreck, great fish, dry land, to turn us back towards the Presence of God from our self-chosen Tarshish. (*TF,* 105–106)

Recalling this belief in the possibility of eternal damnation helps explain both the tones of regret and of urgency that at times are heard in Rossetti's convent poems.

One might, of course, still argue that Rossetti reveals conflicted attitudes about the convent question, for she more often depicts the nun as a troubled woman rather than a woman who is calm and happy in her chosen life. In "The Novice," the speaker is much more concerned about the "poison cup" of earthly love than she is with divine love. Without knowledge of the title, one might see her as another mournful female speaker seeking merely rest from life, especially since there is no mention of God. And as scholars have often noted, "The Convent Threshold" is as much about human love as divine. However, it is important to recall that early in her career as a poet, Rossetti showed an interest in portraying women in moments of spiritual crisis. These convent poems can thus be seen as further evidence of that interest—interest in depicting the spiritual progress of the soul, especially when that soul is housed in a woman's body. Significantly, in three of these poems, the speakers are novices, not fully professed nuns. The title of "The Novice" obviously indicates that fact; the word "threshold" suggests it; and the date 1674, which Rossetti made a point of including in the full title for Soeur Louise's monologue, is the date when Louise de la Vallière entered the convent. (She did not become fully professed until 1675.) Thus, although each speaker has made the decision to renounce the world, Rossetti suggests she has only just begun to climb "the stairs that mount above" (*CP,* 1:61).

Furthermore, when Rossetti arranged her poems for publication, she placed four (she never published "The Novice") so as to emphasize that these women are, in a sense, in progress. In *Goblin Market and Other*

*Poems* (1862), "The Convent Threshold" is placed in the secular section, not the devotional, and more important, it is also placed between "The First Spring Day," a poem as much about the spring "in the world to come" as it is about the earthly season, and "Up-hill," in which a weary soul is comforted by promises of "rest"' Thus, the monologue is not only framed by poems that reinforce and reify, albeit in more moderate tones, the novice's otherworldly perspective, but it is also placed so as to suggest that her spiritual journey is not finished. The road still leads "up-hill all the way" (*CP*, 1:65). In her third volume, *A Pageant and Other Poems* (1881), "Soeur Louise," who, unlike the speaker of "The Convent Threshold," reveals no longing for her former lover, is placed among the devotional poems, but it is not positioned so as to indicate the closure of her spiritual journey. Rather, the poem appears between "A Prodigal Son" and "An 'Immurata' Sister." Thus Rossetti invites the reader to see Sister Louise as a prodigal daughter having just returned to the divine father. Moreover, by placing "An 'Immurata' Sister" immediately after "Soeur Louise," Rossetti implies that Louise has not yet achieved the stage of spiritual growth at which the speaker of "The 'Immurata' Sister" has arrived. Soeur Louise's monologue ends with her bemoaning the destructive power of erotic love: "Oh death-struck love, oh disenkindled fire, / Oh vanity of vanities, desire!" (*CP*, 2:120). In contrast, the immurata sister concludes not with a regret over past earthly loves but with a cry that the fire of divine love fill her soul: "Kindle, flash, my soul; mount higher and higher, / Thou whole burnt-offering!" (2:121).

Because Rossetti never published "Three Nuns," there are no surrounding poems against which to read it; she did, however, place it in her short story *Maude*, where she indicates to the reader that one should indeed see the speakers in different emotional and psychological states. First, by protesting too much, Maude actually associates herself with the first speaker. Although she denies such a comparison, her protests merely serve to draw attention to the similarity between her own world-weariness and that of the first nun. Thus the reader is inclined to see the first nun as still engaged in a spiritual struggle. Maude then claims that the second nun, the one who has fallen in love, "might be Mary had she mistaken her vocation" (60). Such a comment naturally leads the reader to see the second nun as unfit for the convent life. In contrast, Maude asserts that the third is "of course Magdalen" (60), thus leading the reader to see the last speaker in the series as at a stage of spiritual growth far superior to the other two. A close reading of the poem underscores this spiritual hierarchy. The first nun complains of "waiting for the flush of Paradise," and only reluctantly does she follow the devout life. The last stanzas of her monologue reveal that she desires more a return to the "green woods" of childhood innocence than a mystical marriage in heaven. Appropriately, her monologue ends without any anticipation of Paradise, only a hopeless sense of lost innocence:

> There, while yet a child, I thought
> I could live as in a dream,
> Secret, neither found nor sought:
> Till the lilies on the stream,
> Pure as virgin purity,
> Would seem scarce too pure for me:—
> Ah, but that can never be.

(CP, 3:188)

The second nun, however, though still struggling with memories of some unfulfilled and unexpressed earthly love ("We never bartered look for look") concludes her monologue with a request that fellow sisters pray for her soul:

> And pray that I may wake again
> After His likeness, Who hath said
> (Faithful is He who promiseth,)
> We shall be satisfied Therewith.

(3:190)

Unlike the first nun, this woman uses the language of the Bible. These last words intermingle the language of Heb. 10:23 and Ps. 17:15 to tell of Christ's promise that those who come to him will be satisfied. Whereas the first nun looks back to some lost state of innocence, this nun at least looks forward to heavenly reward. However, her recollection of the man she loved indicates that she has not fully achieved the status of a bride of Christ.

The third nun has a true vocation, although being true to that vocation was not always easy: "At first it was a weariness / To watch when once I slept" (3:192). Her sacrifice, however, will lead to spiritual rewards far exceeding anything the earth could offer:

> Lo, in the New Jerusalem
>> Founded and built aright
> My very feet shall tread on light.
>
> (3:191–92)

Like so many of Rossetti's speakers who speak with the voice of authority, she speaks of Last Things. Indeed, the very last line of her monologue quotes Rev. 22:17:

> So now when I am faint, because
>> Hope deferred seems to numb
> My heart, I yet can plead; and say
>> Although my lips are dumb:
> "The Spirit and the Bride say, Come."
>
> (3:193)

Whereas the second nun only hopes for heaven, the third nun speaks with the sure voice of prophesy. She is totally dedicated to the unseen world and to waiting and watching as a bride of Christ. Christian commentators identify "the Bride" in Rev. 22:17 as the church, and clearly Rossetti is suggesting that reading, but in having a nun quote this particular biblical text she also evokes the nuptial imagery associated with the consecrated life. This use of nuptial imagery when writing of nuns might appear as rather conventional and therefore noncontroversial. Certainly, the Roman Catholic Church has long employed such language when speaking of the consecrated life and in the actual investiture of nuns as well. When we consider Rossetti's poems within the context of the revival of Anglican sisterhoods, however, such language places her very much in the midst of the controversy.

Related to the heated objections to the vow of celibacy was a strong opposition to the concept of the celestial marriage between a woman and Christ. For many Victorians, to see a nun as a bride of Christ was not only to challenge woman's proper role as wife and mother but also to elevate the life of celibacy above that of marriage. Those who called for the revival of the conventual life had, at times, done just that. For example, in 1835, when writing in favor of establishing the monastic life within the Church of England, John Henry Newman reminded his readers of the biblical text 1 Cor. 7:34–38, in which Paul discusses the married versus the single life, and concludes, "So then he that giveth her in marriage doeth well; but he that giveth her not in marriage doeth better" (1 Cor. 7:38). However, even among those who supported some type of Protestant religious sisterhood, there were those who could not tolerate such an implication, and accordingly they resisted the biblical interpretation that read the Pauline text as elevating the celibate life over marriage. For example, Frederick Maurice, a clergyman who was willing to praise a newly formed nursing sisterhood (probably the Society of All Saints) for doing useful work, argued that Paul had not "undervalued married in comparison with single life," and not surprisingly, therefore, Maurice viewed "the idea of the vow [of celibacy] as the contract of an individual soul to the celestial Bridegroom [as] subversive of the principle of the Catholic Church, denying the dignity, annulling the obligations of other Christians."[21]

When writing her early poems such as "Three Nuns," Rossetti may not have been aware of the intense opposition to the vow of celibacy and the nuptial imagery associated with it. Certainly, however, by the time her friend Reverend Littledale, who was himself associated with the Sisterhood of St. Margaret, asked her to write a hymn for the profession of a nun, she must have known quite well that many of her contemporaries, even many within the Anglican Church, could not accept elevating celibacy above marriage. Rossetti did not date the hymn she wrote; however, it does not appear in her 1866 collection *Prince's Progress and Other Poems* but is included in the devotional section of her 1875 collection, which suggests that the composition date is the late 1860s or the early 1870s. By that point, not only was the debate over Anglican convents fully underway, but Maria Rossetti had also begun her association with All Saints. Significantly, the poem Rossetti composed, "'The Master Is

---

21. John Henry Newman, "Letters on the Church of the Fathers, no. XII," *British Magazine* 6 (June 1835): 663; Rev. Frederick D. Maurice, "On Sisterhoods," *Victorian Magazine* 1 (August 1863): 301.

Come, and Calleth for Thee,'" not only employs the imagery of the celestial marriage but makes it central to the whole poem. Although each stanza is structured around a relationship between the woman being addressed in the poem, presumably the nun, and God—beginning with that of father and daughter, followed by master and disciple, monarch and subject, lord and creature—the poem culminates in the image of the woman as Christ's bride:

> Who calleth?—The Bridegroom calleth,
>     Soar, O Bride with the Seraphim:
> He Who loves thee as no man loveth,
>     Bids thee give up thy heart to Him.

(CP, 1:226)

Rossetti associates this woman, who is to give her heart to God, with the seraphim, those classified as the highest order of angels and those described by Isaiah as having three pairs of wings. Moreover, in this poem, God's love is placed clearly above that of man, and thus Rossetti suggests this woman is indeed choosing to do "better" by remaining single.

Further insight into Rossetti's reading of the controversial Pauline text can be found by turning to her devotional prose. In her book of prayers, *Annus Domini*, one finds the following prayer: "O Lord Jesus Christ, the Bridegroom, I entreat Thee, give us all grace to hear Thy Voice; that married persons may love Thee in each other, and each other in Thee; and that the unmarried, keeping themselves from sin, may love Thee without let or hindrance throughout time and through eternity" (*AD*, 181). This prayer suggests that Rossetti found in 1 Cor. 7:34 ("The unmarried woman careth for the things of the Lord, that she may be holy both in body and in spirit: but she that is married careth for the things of the world, how she may please her husband") the message that a woman who remained unmarried would have the potential of a more direct experience of God than the woman who married. In *Letter and Spirit*, in a passage in which Rossetti considers the two figures of "the married woman and the virgin" as "illustrative of the First and Second Commandments," she makes explicit this view:

> She whose heart is virginal abides aloft and aloof in spirit. In
> spirit she often times kneels rather than sits, or prostrates herself

more readily than she kneels, associated by love with Seraphim, and echoing and swelling the "Holy, Holy, Holy" of their perpetual adoration. Her spiritual eyes behold the King in His beauty: wherefore she forgets by comparison, her own people and her father's house. Her Maker is her Husband, endowing her with a name better than of sons and daughters. . . .

The Wife's case, not in unison with that other, yet makes a gracious harmony with it. She sees not face to face, but as it were in a glass darkly. Every thing, and more than all every person, and most of all the one best beloved person [her husband] becomes her mirror wherein she beholds Christ and her shrine wherein she serves Him. (*LS*, 91–92)

Although Rossetti concludes this comparison with a remark in regard to the dangers of each "holy estate" ("the Virgin tends to become narrow, self-centred; the Wife to worship and serve the creature more than the Creator" [94]), her use of biblical allusion suggests a hierarchy of voices: a dutiful Christian wife sees God "in a glass darkly" while the virginal heart sees, with her "spiritual eyes," the King. Rossetti associates the wife with the Pauline verse regarding mortal life (see 1 Cor. 13:12), whereas the virgin is associated with Isa. 33:17, a text that speaks of the faithful of Israel who shall behold the Lord. Clearly, for a woman of her time, Rossetti held a very atypical attitude toward marriage. Indeed, in her last work of devotional prose, she is even willing openly to challenge the Victorian celebration of motherhood when she questions Rachel's plea to Jacob for children: "'Give me children, or else I die,' was a foolish speech: the childless who make themselves nursing mothers of Christ's little ones are true mothers in Israel" (*FD*, 312).

Rossetti's questioning of the Victorian celebration of marriage and motherhood might lead to a reading of her convent poems as support for woman's political rights. Indeed, scholarship on the history of Anglican sisterhoods strongly suggests that their establishment can be seen "as part of a larger 'silent rebellion' against Victorian restrictions on women," and that such sisterhoods offered a woman a "privileged space" within which she could develop a useful career of service.[22] An unmarried woman in

22. Reed, "A Female Movement," 229–30.

Victorian England might actually be seen to have had more independence and power within an Anglican sisterhood than if she had remained a dependent in her father's or brother's household. However, while Rossetti's nuns, especially when depicted as brides of Christ, directly challenge the Victorian domestic ideology, they only indirectly question patriarchal restrictions on women's rights. For it is important to recall that Rossetti's nuns are shown not asserting independence in the world but asserting a right to renounce the world so that they might better devote themselves to God. If one argues that these women seek freedom, one must also recognize that such freedom is sought so that they might better sacrifice the self to Divine Love.

As scholars and biographers have repeatedly noted, renunciation is one of Rossetti's major themes.[23] How this theme is presented often depends largely on the dominant ideas and values of the critic's own time and, in some cases, the critic's own religious views. For example, Katharine Tynan, who was herself a devout Roman Catholic and a writer of religious verse, writes, "I think in spite of the human passion which beats through much of her poetry she was of the women who are called to be Brides of Christ, own sister of St. Teresa and St. Catherine of Siena." Tynan obviously belongs to the early period of Rossetti scholarship, when the poet was to be seen as a saint. Sandra M. Gilbert and Susan Gubar, on the other hand, are among those who have shaped one of the more recent images, that of Rossetti as the repressed victim of the patriarchy. Employing in their criticism a feminist approach influenced by psychoanalytic views, they see what they term Rossetti's "aesthetic of renunciation" as having stifled her creative potential, and they imply that Rossetti would have written more powerful verse if she had not adopted a humble feminine voice: Rather than describe her as a bride of Christ, they speak of her as "bury[ing] herself alive in a coffin of renunciation."[24]

Some recent scholars have resisted both these images of Rossetti by

23. For example, see Conrad Festa, "Renunciation in Christina Rossetti's Poetry," *Pre-Raphaelite Review* 3 (May 1980): 25–35; and Jerome Bump, "Christina Rossetti and the Pre-Raphaelite Brotherhood," in *The Achievement of Christina Rossetti*, ed. David A. Kent (Ithaca: Cornell University Press, 1987), 336.

24. Katharine Tynan, "Santa Christina," *Bookman* 41 (January 1912): 189; Sandra M. Gilbert and Susan Gubar, *The Madwoman in the Attic: The Woman Writer and the Nineteenth-Century Literary Imagination* (New Haven: Yale University Press, 1979), 587, 558.

placing emphasis on historical context. Kathleen Blake, for example, argues that renunciation of romantic love not only gave a Victorian woman writer a subject but also created a situation that both allowed her and motivated her to write. And Antony Harrison emphasizes that Rossetti's renunciatory stance toward the world "operates as a powerful cultural critique" of the Victorian patriarchal society.[25] Although both these readings offer very helpful correctives to the earlier interpretations of this stance, I would like to stress the importance of placing Rossetti's nuns and nunlike personas within the context of the full system of belief she embraced. Otherwise, one might be inclined to see Rossetti as a Victorian woman who assumed a renunciatory stance only so that she might feel empowered during an age that restricted the feminine sphere. Certainly, her faith must have brought her comfort and consolation, but to cast it only in such terms is to present her faith more as a device for coping with reality than as the reality it was to her. Moreover, viewing the renunciatory theme in isolation from the whole of her faith tends to enlarge its importance. For Rossetti, controlling bodily and worldly appetites was an important stage in the quest for holiness; it was not an end in itself. Too often, critics have overlooked the hopeful and joyous messages also to be found in Rossetti's religious verse.

One should first consider what Rossetti meant by "the world." First, she often presents the world, as she does in her famous poem "The World," as an embodiment of the deceptive qualities of all physical beauty and pleasure that tempts the individual to sell his or her soul for the false promise of "ripe fruits, sweet flowers, and full satiety" (CP, 1:77). The promise is, of course, false because for Rossetti, nothing in this life can fully satisfy the longing one feels; full satiety can only be known in heaven. To underscore that belief, Rossetti also repeatedly dwells on the temporal nature of this world, as, for example, in her numerous poems stressing the vanity of this life. Yet although Rossetti does indeed repeatedly remind her readers that this life is "passing away," and while an ascetic strain can be found throughout her work, the theme of *vanitas mundi,* so apparent in her early poems, is tempered in her later

---

25. Kathleen Blake, *Love and the Woman Question in Victorian Literature: The Art of Self-Postponement* (Totowa, N.J.: Barnes and Noble, 1983), ix–x; Harrison, *Christina Rossetti in Context,* 188.

writings by a limited acceptance of the world. In other words, she speaks of the world not only as "mouldy, worm-eaten, grey," as in her poem "'A Vain Shadow,'" but also as a place to work. Exactly when her thoughts altered is hard to date precisely. A few poems written in the late 1850s, such as "'I have a message unto thee,'" "Another Spring," and especially "'What good shall my life do me'" suggest that Rossetti began during those years to reconsider her earlier negative vision of the world. Certainly, by the time of her later devotional prose, she is reminding her readers that while this world should never be seen as home, it is the place one must work to earn heaven: "This world is not my orchard for fruit or my garden for flowers. It is however my only field whence to raise a harvest" (*FD*, 333). Furthermore, as Rossetti continues her commentary, she concludes that this world is dangerous not because it in itself is corrupt and evil but because it is the place where evil has access to the human soul:

> What is the world? Wherein resides its harmfulness, snare, pollution? Left to itself it is neither harmful, ensnaring, nor polluting. It becomes all this as the passive agent, passive vehicle if I may so call it, of the devil, man's outside tempter, and the flesh, man's inside tempter. There is no inherent evil in cedar and vermillion, horses and chariots, purple and fine linen; nay, nor in sumptuous fare, in down, silk, apes, ivory, or peacocks. St Peter himself objects not to hair, gold apparel, but to women's misuse of them. An alabaster box of precious ointment becomes good or bad simply according to the use it is put to. Through envy of the devil death came into the world, and man hath sought out many inventions; but the heavens and the earth, and all the host of them when made and finished were beheld as "very good." (333)

As is typical of both her prose and poetic style, Rossetti weaves multiple biblical allusions throughout this passage. However, she concludes by drawing the reader's attention to the last verse of Gen. 1: "And God saw every thing that he had made, and, behold, it was very good." Creation itself is good; it is the "many inventions" of human beings that are not always good. In other words, it is the use of and response to the things of the world that endanger the soul. In *Seek and Find*, Rossetti offers a clear statement of how she believes human beings should respond to creation: "It is good for us to enjoy all good things which fall to our temporal lot, so long as such enjoyment kindles and feeds the desire of better things reserved for our eternal inheritance. The younger fairer than the elder (Judges xv.2), the best wine last (St. John ii.10), these are symbols calculated to set us while on earth hankering, longing, straining, after heaven" (*SF*, 180–81). Because of the first sin of Adam and Eve, the world was fallen, but as long as the beauties and joys of this world led the soul to long for the full satisfaction to be known in heaven, as long as they were read as symbols of the divine, then in Rossetti eyes, neither the beauty nor the pleasure in that beauty was tainted.

When considering the renunciatory stance in Rossetti's poetry, it is also essential to recall that for Rossetti, renunciation of worldly pleasure was only a part of the spiritual journey; the goal was always heaven. Therefore, in reading Rossetti's poems that urge the reader to renounce the world or to beware the temptations of the world, one must keep in mind her belief in a reward of individual immortality and spiritual joy. Rossetti implies such a view in the emphasis she places on the afterlife in almost all of her convent poems and in several other poems of suffering and sacrifice, poems written throughout her career, such as "The Lowest Room" (1856), "From House to Home" (1858), "Martyr's Song" (1863), "'They Desire a Better Country'" (before 1875), "A Martyr" (before 1881), and "Ballad of Boding" (before 1881). In each of these poems, she offers her readers not only the imagery of suffering but also that of the glorious world of the redeemed. "Ballad of Boding," for example, ends with a description of the third ship, the one rowed by those who knew "no feast," "steer[ing] into the splendours of the sky":

That third bark and that least
Which had never seemed to feast,
Yet kept high festival above sun and moon and star.

(*CP*, 2:85)

The implication is clear: renunciation in this life leads to joy in the next.

In her devotional prose, Rossetti makes this belief explicitly clear. For example, in *Letter and Spirit*, she writes: "True, all our lives long we shall be bound to refrain our soul and keep it low: but what then? For the books we now forbear to read, we shall one day be endued with wisdom and knowledge. For the music we will not listen to, we shall join in the song of the redeemed. . . . For the pleasures we miss, we shall abide, and for evermore abide, in the rapture of heaven" (104). And in *Called to Be Saints*, she offers her readers one of her most personal expressions on the subject of renunciation and reward:

> When it seems (as sometimes through revulsion of feeling and urgency of Satan it may seem) that our yoke is uneasy and our burden unbearable, because our life is pared down and subdued and repressed to an intolerable level: and so in one moment every instinct of our whole self revolts against our lot, and we loathe this day of quietness and of sitting still, and writhe under a sudden sense of all we have irrecoverably foregone, of the right hand, or foot, or eye cast from us, of the haltingness and maimedness of our entrance (if enter we do at last) into life,—then the Seraphim of Isaiah's vision making music in our memory revive hope in our heart.
> (*CS*, 435)

After comforting her readers with reference to Isaiah's vision (see Isa. 6:2–4), Rossetti then elaborates on that vision by stressing how in heaven one will find a complete reversal of the condition one has known on earth:

> For at the sound of their mighty cry of full-flooding adoration, the very posts of the door moved and the house was filled with smoke. No lack there, nothing subdued there; no bridle, no curb, no self-sacrifice: outburst of sympathy, fulness of joy, pleasures for evermore, likeness that satisfieth; beauty for ashes, oil of joy for mourning, the garment of praise for the spirit of heaviness; things new out of God's treasure-house,—things old also, please God. 'My sons, give Me thy heart,' He saith, and accepteth blessing it. 'Give Me thy son,' He saith also; and accepts and hides our darling; but one day gives him back to us. (435–36)

When reading any of Rossetti's poems on the suffering in this life occasioned by the need to renounce some earthly pleasure, we should keep in mind that she believed in this glorious world of satisfaction and joy, a place where even the beloved who had died would be seen again.

If we return to Rossetti's poems of nuns and nunlike heroines, with this image of an eternal life of recompense for all sacrificed on earth, we can see clearly that Rossetti did not support the Anglican sisterhoods for political or practical reasons, but for spiritual reasons. In Rossetti's eyes, the Anglican sisterhoods were far more than communities of social workers, and more than communities of redundant women seeking power and freedom in a patriarchal world. In Rossetti's mind, a woman who chose "the stairs that mount above" did so in order to one day "soar" with the seraphim. Throughout Rossetti's lifetime, the nun was to her an image of the soul renouncing any desire for power in this world in order to win a crown in paradise. Thus while Rossetti's respect for the conventual life does not directly support woman's political emancipation on earth, it does affirm a woman's right to reject the title of wife if she feels the Master has come and called for her.

Rossetti clearly saw the woman with a genuine religious vocation as having achieved a lofty spiritual status while still on earth, but she certainly does not ever suggest that the consecrated religious life is suitable for all. In *The Face of the Deep*, after commenting on "chaste virgins" who "choose solitude for bower" so as to be able to remain "unsullied" by this life, she turns her thoughts to Adam and Eve: "Nevertheless, however good for the present distress [life in this world], yet from the beginning God Himself declared that it is not good for man to be alone" (93). Though Rossetti turned to the convent for subject matter, she more often examined human relationships outside convent walls.

*three*

# THE CHRISTIAN FAIRY-TALE POEMS

☨

NOT ONLY DID ROSSETTI CONSIDER THE CONSECRATED SINGLE
life spiritually superior to married life, but numerous poems, especially
those written during the 1850–1870 period, strongly suggest that she
viewed the institution of marriage with a cynical eye. For example, in
"Love from the North" (1856), "The Hour and the Ghost" (1856),
"Maggie a Lady" (1865), and "Husband and Wife" (1865), love and
marriage seem at odds, for love is threatened by marriage or marriage by
love. In other poems, such as "Lowest Room" (1856), "Maude Clare"
(1858), "Sister Maude" (1860), "Noble Sisters" (1860), "Last Night"
(1863), and "A Ring Posy"(1863), Rossetti explores the destructive female rivalry that emerges when a society places primary importance on a
woman's marital status. And as we shall see in Chapter 4, during these
years Rossetti also writes her fallen woman ballads, in which she questions the wife's dominant position in the Victorian female hierarchy by
blurring distinctions between pure and fallen. As several critics have convincingly argued, Rossetti's poems on love and marriage challenge the
patriarchal ideology of her time and suggest that she was, especially during the 1850s and 1860s, engaging in a harsh analysis of Victorian marriage.[1] Although Rossetti indeed viewed the Victorian marriage market

---

1. See, for example, Ronald D. Morrison, " 'One droned in sweetness like a fattened

as a place of competition and betrayal, such a cynical view does not represent the full range of her thoughts on human love, or even on marriage. For example, "Goblin Market" (1859) and "Maiden-Song" (1863), two of her most significant narrative poems, close with the traditional marriage ending, and in both poems sisterly love, not rivalry, is central in bringing about the final domestic scenes.

Significantly, Rossetti links these two poems together in her 1875 collected edition, which gave her the opportunity of combining poems from her previous two volumes, *Goblin Market and Other Poems* and *The Prince's Progress and Other Poems,* into a new arrangement. In this 1875 volume, Rossetti places "Goblin Market" first, followed by her second title poem, "The Prince's Progress," which is followed by "Maiden-Song." ("Maiden-Song" was also paired with "The Prince's Progress" in the 1866 edition.) Together these three poems form a complementary series in which Rossetti uses the secular form of the fairy tale and the signs and symbols of Christianity to explore not only how human love might hinder one's spiritual development but also how it might help. Looking at these three poems, separately and as a series, suggests that as Rossetti matured (in 1875 she was forty-five years old), she was attempting to offer her readers, especially her women readers, not only warnings about the spiritual dangers of earthly love but also lessons in how human love, both sisterly love and married love, might take on, as she later phrased it when writing her devotional diary, *Time Flies,* a "tinge of heaven" (132).

Numerous readings of "Goblin Market" have been offered, employing various critical approaches. For example, this poem of innocent maidens and sinister goblins has been read as a story of temptation and redemption, as an autobiographical narrative revealing repressed sexuality, a critique of Victorian materialism, a rejection of patriarchal amatory values, a celebration of woman's power, a sexual fantasy of incestuous lesbian love, and a literary representation of the eating disorder anorexia

bee': Christina Rossetti's View of Marriage in Her Early Poetry," *Kentucky Philological Review* 5 (1990): 19–26; Jerome J. McGann, "Christina Rossetti's Poems: A New Edition and a Revaluation," *Victorian Studies* 23 (1980): 237–54; Antony H. Harrison, *Christina Rossetti in Context* (Chapel Hill: University of North Carolina Press, 1988), 112–25; Katherine J. Mayberry, *Christina Rossetti and the Poetry of Discovery* (Baton Rouge: Louisiana State University Press, 1989), 55–58.

nervosa.[2] Although these various readings attest to the richness of the poem, too often the numerous allusions to Christianity are simply ignored or quickly dismissed.[3] Thus, a poem so clearly about body and soul is often read as focusing only on the body, and the powerful and even subversive message Rossetti offers her Victorian readers regarding human love and female spirituality remains unnoticed.

In general, critics agree that the central symbol of "Goblin Market" is the fruit, which the goblins describe at length and in sensuous terms: "Plump unpecked cherries . . . Wild free-born cranberries" (*CP,* 1:11). For those who see the poem as focusing on the female body, these descriptions appealing to the eye, and through the eyes to the taste, are to be read not only in sensual terms but in sexual terms. In other words, the fruit is seen as representing forbidden sexual experience, especially experience forbidden to unmarried Victorian women.[4] However, if we read these lines with Rossetti's Christian faith in mind, they point not to the pleasure to be experienced in satisfying any of the sensual appetites, but rather to the impossibility of ever finding full satisfaction by attempting to satisfy the body. In Ecclesiastes, the Preacher develops his warning of earth's vanities by reminding his readers that "the eye is not satisfied with seeing, nor the ear filled with hearing" (Eccles. 1:8). More important, St. Paul, who is echoing Isa. 64:3, also assures the Corinthians that the glo-

2. For a very useful listing of the numerous articles on "Goblin Market," see Jane Addison, "Christina Rossetti Studies, 1974–1991: A Checklist and Synthesis," *Bulletin of Bibliography* 2 (March 1995): 89–92.

3. For recent readings of "Goblin Market" that do focus on Rossetti's faith, see Mary Arseneau, "Incarnation and Interpretation: Christina Rossetti, and the Oxford Movement, and 'Goblin Market,'" *Victorian Poetry* 31 (spring 1993): 79–93; Linda E. Marshall, "'Transfigured to His Likeness': Sensible Transcendentalism in Christina Rossetti's 'Goblin Market,'" *University of Toronto Quarterly* 63 (spring 1994): 429–50; and Linda Peterson, "Restoring the Book: The Typological Hermeneutics of Christina Rossetti and the PRB," *Victorian Poetry* 32 (autumn–winter 1994): 209–27. I am indebted to these three articles for helping me to clarify my reading of the poem.

4. For example, see Germaine Greer, Introduction to *Goblin Market* by Christina Rossetti (New York: Stonehill, 1975), vii–xxxvi; Cora Kaplan, "The Indefinite Disclosed: Christina Rossetti and Emily Dickinson," in *Women Writing and Writing About Women,* ed. Mary Jacobus (New York: Barnes and Noble, 1979), 61–79; and Margaret Homans, "'Syllables of Velvet': Dickinson, Rossetti, and the Rhetorics of Sexuality," *Feminist Studies* 11 (fall 1985): 569–93.

ries of heaven are beyond anything the senses can perceive: "But as it is written, Eye hath not seen, nor ear heard, neither have entered into the heart of man, the things which God hath prepared for them that love him" (1 Cor. 2:9). Rossetti often weaves this particular Pauline text into her own devotional poetry, as in "Eye Hath Not Seen" (1852) and "Advent" (1858). To a reader familiar with biblical allusion and language, Rossetti's sensuous descriptions immediately signal a spiritual warning. Such a reader immediately realizes that the goblins are not primarily interested in Laura's body. Rather, through the seduction of the body, they hope to destroy her soul.

Significantly, once Laura's physical eyes are satisfied, clear signs appear that her soul is in danger. First, she no longer speaks of the possible evil origins of the fruit, as she did previously, but imagines a fair world: "How fair the vine must grow / Whose grapes are so luscious" (*CP*, 1:12). Later, after her goblin feast, she even imagines that she has tasted fruit that will end all human sorrow. She assures Lizzie, "Have done with sorrow / I'll bring you plums tomorrow" (1:15). In her religious poetry and devotional prose, Rossetti repeatedly reminds her readers that only God ends sorrow, and only in paradise will "tears [be] wiped from tearful eyes" ("Three Nuns," *CP*, 3:191). For one who shares Rossetti's faith, Laura's claim to Lizzie is not only a sign of foolish pride but a sign that she has mistaken the sensual for the spiritual.

Both the fact that Laura sees the fruit as pleasing and her disregard for the limits placed upon her recall the first woman who turned from God: Eve. Rossetti's interpretation of Eve is discussed at length in Chapter 5; however, it is appropriate to mention at this point that Rossetti did not see the fall of humankind in sexual terms. For Rossetti, Eve's sin was primarily one of disobedience, not sexual lust.

Although much of what Rossetti writes on sin and redemption appears in her devotional prose, which was written after "Goblin Market," placing this poem within the context of these later works sheds light on the general tendency of her thoughts. Such texts are especially helpful in furthering our understanding of Rossetti's symbolic use of sensuous goblin fruit. Especially significant is what Rossetti writes in *Letter and Spirit* about the Second Commandment, a commandment she sees as "adapted especially to man as compounded of soul and body" (69–70). As Rossetti develops her discussion, she associates all sensual temptations with this commandment against the worship of "graven images":

> I think we may venture to consider not merely that each infringement of the Second Commandment must necessarily (so to say) have its bodily as well as its spiritual characteristic, but that all temptations whatsoever which harass us through our senses and could obtain no access to us at all except through our sensual side,—that all such temptations may be classed as warring against the Second Commandment; and that all and any yielding to such temptations involves a breach of that same Second Commandment. This assumed, the Sixth, Seventh, and Eighth Commandments appear as correlatives of the Second Commandment. . . .
> Allowing thus much, it follows that our breach of the Second Commandment consists in substituting in our affections and homage some thing, any thing for God. (*LS*, 70–71)

Thus, to see Laura as guilty of indulging in forbidden sexual pleasure when she eats the goblin fruit need not be excluded from a religious reading of "Goblin Market." However, keeping what Rossetti writes about the Second Commandment in mind, we see Laura not just as a woman who has committed some sexual sin, but rather as a figure of all those who place sensual gratification of any kind before God.[5]

Significantly, in the description of Laura's response to her goblin feast, Rossetti provides an explicit sign that Laura has indeed done just that: Laura believes that the goblin fruit is "Sweeter than honey from the rock." Such a comparison echoes Ps. 81:16: "And with honey out of the rock should I have satisfied thee." In the language of Christian symbolism, the rock is read as a reference to Christ. Rossetti herself offers such a reading in *Seek and Find*: "Thus not sun and star alone set Him forth: but the rock symbolizes His unfailing strength (St. Matt. vii. 24, 25); and is all the more like Him when it yields refreshment (Ex. viii. 5, 6; 1 Cor. x. 4), or sweetness" (260). Not surprisingly, after Laura's feast, we are told

---

5. For further evidence that Rossetti came to see all sin as in some way a sin of idolatry, see her discussion of sin in *The Face of the Deep* (251, 397), and her comments on idolatry in *Seek and Find* (51).

that "her tree of life drooped from the root." In Revelation, the tree of life is promised "to him that overcometh" (Rev. 2:7), in other words, to those who follow Christ and his commandments. Laura's physical decline is to be read as emblematic of a spiritual one, and if she is not reconciled to God, she will become quite literally a lost soul. She will follow the path of Jeanie, who ate goblin fruit and who now lies in a barren grave. In general, no matter the critical methodology applied, critics have interpreted Jeanie as representing a Victorian fallen woman:

> She [Lizzie] thought of Jeanie in her grave,
> Who should have been a bride;
> But who for joys brides hope to have
> Fell sick and died
> In her gay prime.

> (CP, 1:19)

However, if we keep Rossetti's views on the commandments in mind, Jeanie becomes not simply guilty of sins of sexual lust but guilty of idolatry, guilty of placing the things of the world before God. In a sense, Jeanie can be read as suggestive of the Israel of the Old Testament, which should have been God's bride but which was cursed with barrenness when it "play[ed] the harlot," that is, when it turned from the true God to worship idols (see Jer. 2:20; Isa. 5:6–24). Certainly, Rossetti is evoking images of sensuality in both Laura's goblin feast and employing metaphors of sexuality in reference to Jeanie, but she is using them as such metaphors are often used in the Old Testament, that is, to refer to the soul and its relationship to the one true God.

It might also be argued, as Linda Marshall suggests, that the phrase "joys brides hope to have" is not to be read as a reference to the sexual consummation of marriage but rather to the offspring born as the result of such a consummation, in other words, to "motherhood."[6] Indeed, Rossetti's poem "The Flowers Appear on the Earth," which privileges the flowers placed on graves, symbols of "[long] love and resurrection," above those of the bride, underscores the perceptiveness of Marshall's reading. In this poem written four years before "Goblin Market," Ros-

---

6. Marshall, "'Transfigured to His Likeness,'" 440.

setti warns the young bride that her "hoped-for sweet / May yet outstrip her feet" (*CP*, 2:320). Such a warning clearly is not referring to the sexual consummation of the marriage bed but rather to the hopes for a pleasant worldly life, a life defined for a young nineteenth-century woman in terms of a happy marriage and family. Clearly, to read the figure of Jeanie merely as a Victorian fallen woman is too limiting.

Rossetti's commentary on the commandments also provides insight into the reading of Lizzie's character, the sister who is properly suspicious of the things that appeal to the senses. In response to Laura's cry to "look" at goblin men, she refuses adamantly and warns her sister of the danger: "'No,' said Lizzie: 'No, no, no; / Their offers should not charm us'" (*CP*, 1:12). At this moment, Lizzie keeps the Second Commandment. However, later she also follows the commandments of the New Testament as well. Significantly, in *Letter and Spirit*, Rossetti begins not with a listing of the Ten Commandments of the Old Testament, but the two as given by Christ: "Hear O Israel; The Lord our God is one Lord: and though shalt love the Lord thy God with all thy heart, and with all thy soul, and with all thy mind, and with all thy strength," and "Thou shalt love thy neighbour as thyself" (Mark 12:20–31) (*LS*, 5).

Lizzie's response to goblin fruit, which involves a hurried flight from the goblin men, results unintentionally in her sister's being left alone; later, however, when she sees Laura's suffering, Lizzie acts in accordance with the second of Christ's commandments. First, Lizzie seeks to "share" Laura's "cankerous care" (*CP*, 1:19). Then, when Laura grows increasingly worse, Lizzie stops being afraid of the cost and prepares to meet the goblins: "And for the first time in her life / Began to listen and look" (1:19). It is important to note that she begins "to listen and look" for the sake of someone she loves, not to satisfy her curiosity. Furthermore, she is never tempted by the pleasing appearance of the fruit. When the goblins try to make her eat, she resists:

> They trod and hustled her,
> Elbowed and jostled her,
> Clawed with their nails,
> Barking, mewing, hissing, mocking,
> Tore her gown and soiled her stocking,
> Twitched her hair out by the roots,

Stamped upon her tender feet,
Held her hands and squeezed their fruits
Against her mouth to make her eat.

(1:21)

Not surprisingly, critics who read the poem as a narrative of sexual experience see the goblin attack as attempted rape. Some argue that this encounter is an important stage in Lizzie's growth into womanhood, for it leads her to face her fear of her own sexuality.[7] However, while Rossetti well might have been consciously evoking the image of rape, the lines describing Lizzie's resistance suggest that this assault, one suffered for the sake of another, is a stage in Lizzie's spiritual, not sexual, development:

White and golden Lizzie stood,
Like a lily in a flood,—
Like a rock of blue-veined stone
Lashed by tides obstreperously,—
Like a beacon left alone
In a hoary roaring sea,
Sending up a golden fire,—
Like a fruit-crowned orange-tree
White with blossoms honey-sweet
Sore beset by wasp and bee,—
Like a royal virgin town
Topped with gilded dome and spire
Close beleaguered by a fleet
Mad to tug her standard down.

(1:21–22)

This list of similes in which Lizzie is compared to a lily, a rock, a beacon, a blossoming fruit tree, and a royal town can all be read within the context of Christian symbolism. For example, in Christian art, both the lily and orange blossoms are used as emblems of the purity of the Virgin

7. For example, see Janet Galligani Casey, "The Potential of Sisterhood: Christina Rossetti's 'Goblin Market,'" *Victorian Poetry* 29 (spring 1991): 69.

Mary.[8] A rock, signifying stability, and a beacon, suggestive of light, are often associated with either Christ and/or the Christian church. In *The Face of the Deep*, Rossetti's description of the Church Militant actually echoes this scene of assault:

> The Church Militant sojourns in "this world," whereof Christ declared: "The prince of this world cometh, and hath nothing in Me." Thus abides she within the enemy's camp, finding there no rest for the sole of her foot. Howbeit, in accordance with that great prophetic promise which our Lord vouchsafed to St. Peter, she is set upon a rock where the gates of hell shall not prevail against her. She stands as a city that is set on an hill, as a besieged city, compassed together on every side, hostile hosts swarming about her like bees. (111)

Just as the Church Militant does not succumb to evil, neither does Lizzie. Indeed, Lizzie's successful confrontation with the goblin men strengthens her soul. As she runs home, the narrator makes it clear that Lizzie is not running out of fear but out of satisfaction that she has won the "fiery antidote" for her sister: "The kind heart made her windy-paced / That urged her home quite out of breath with haste / And inward laughter" (*CP*, 1:23). The obedient maiden, who first knew when to flee evil, now also proves herself to be a maiden who can face and resist evil for another's sake. In other words, she becomes a figure of self-sacrificing love, and thus she becomes a figure of Christ Himself. Rossetti underscores Lizzie's Christ-likeness, in her call to Laura, which recalls Christ's words to his apostles at the Last Supper:

> "Eat me, drink me, love me;
> Laura, make much of me;
> For your sake I have braved the glen
> And had to do with goblin merchant men."

(*CP*, 1:23)

---

8. George Ferguson, *Signs and Symbols in Christian Art* (New York: Oxford University Press, 1954), 41, 44–45; Alice M. Coats, *Flowers and Their Histories* (New York: Pitman Publishing 1956), 142–43.

The series of images Rossetti employs in developing Lizzie's character is not unorthodox, for Christian theology teaches that each individual soul reflects the Church Militant and that the Church reflects Christ. However, Rossetti's placing before her Victorian audience such a clear working out of these Christian beliefs has a subversive element. There is nothing unusual for a Victorian audience in Rossetti's depiction of Lizzie as the Church Militant, for the church is traditionally characterized as feminine, but when Rossetti associates Lizzie with Christ, she blurs the sharp gender distinctions of the nineteenth century. For example, a reader who sees Lizzie as mirroring Christ might then either recognize the feminine aspect in Christ's sacrifice of self or see Lizzie's sisterly sacrifice in masculine terms, that is, might see Lizzie as acting not like a heroine but a hero. Second, by employing a female character as a Christ figure, Rossetti challenges those Victorian readers who, in a society that regarded women as inferior creatures, might easily have disregarded woman's spiritual equality with men. Although Rossetti accepted that women could not become priests, she nevertheless heard in the New Testament a clear call to all, men and women, to become like Christ: "Every Christian is in his *or her* degree Veronica (true Image) of Christ" (*FD*, 329; emphasis mine). Many twentieth-century readers have found the Eucharistic scene between the two sisters startling because of what they perceive as a portrayal of female sexuality, but the Victorians well may have been startled because of its portrayal of female spirituality.[9] Victorian women were to be moral guides; nevertheless, the language and iconography used by Victorians who encourage or support that behavior more often associate women with angels, who purify the home through gentleness and patient endurance.[10] Typically, Victorian literature and art do not depict women as Christ-like saviors who can enter the "haunted glen," resist a goblin attack, and "win the fiery antidote."

Various readings of "Goblin Market" draw attention to Lizzie as a

9. For an insightful discussion of female relationships in the nineteenth century, see Carol Smith-Rosenberg, "The Female World of Love and Ritual: Relations Between Women in Nineteenth-Century America," *Signs* 1 (autumn–winter 1975): 1–29.

10. For a discussion of woman's role as a moral guide in Victorian literature and art, see Debra N. Mancoff, *The Return of King Arthur: The Legend Through Victorian Eyes* (New York: Harry N. Abrams, 1995), 72–99; and Susan P. Casteras, *Images of Victorian Womanhood in English Art* (Cranbury, N.J.: Associated University Presses, 1987).

Christ figure. No one, however, has yet given any detailed attention to Rossetti's Eucharistic beliefs.[11] Some understanding of these beliefs is certainly necessary for a full appreciation of the scene so many twentieth-century critics have read in merely sensual terms.

As a devout Anglican, Rossetti would not have accepted the Roman Catholic doctrine of transubstantiation; however, she would have viewed Holy Communion as far more than a commemoration of the Last Supper. Recalling what the Book of Common Prayer states on this subject is instructive: "The Supper of the Lord is not only a sign of the love that Christians ought to have among themselves one to another; but rather is a Sacrament of our Redemption by Christ's death: insomuch that to such as rightly, worthily, and with faith, receive the same, the Bread which we break is a partaking of the Body of Christ; and likewise the cup of Blessing is a partaking of the Blood of Christ."[12] Although considerable debate occurred in the nineteenth century over the interpretation of this particular article of faith, in general Anglican theologians, especially those of the High Church, read it as supporting the doctrine of the real presence, that is, the doctrine asserting that Christ is indeed present during the service of Holy Communion either in the consecrated bread and wine or in the heart of the faithful receiver.[13]

There is nothing in Rossetti's devotional poetry or prose that suggests she ever doubted this doctrine, and repeatedly she reminds her readers that in receiving Holy Communion one is brought into direct contact with God. For example, in *Time Flies,* she refers to "that 'Bread and Wine' whereby the faithful receive verily and indeed 'the Body and

11. For readings that see Lizzie as a redeemer, see James Ashcroft Noble, "Christina Rossetti," *Literary Opinion* (December 1891): 156; Marian Shalkhauser, "The Feminine Christ," *Victorian Newsletter* 10 (autumn 1956): 19–20; and Sylvia Bailey Shurbutt, "Revisionist Mythmaking in Christina Rossetti's 'Goblin Market': Eve's Apple and Other Questions Revised and Reconsidered," *Victorian Newsletter* 82 (fall 1992): 40–44. Arseneau and Marshall also note Lizzie's Christlike behavior.

12. In seeking to understand Rossetti's views on the Eucharist, I have relied on her own devotional poetry and prose; The Book of Common Prayer; Peter Benedict Nockles, *The Oxford Movement in Context: Anglican High Churchmanship, 1760–1857* (Cambridge: Cambridge University Press, 1994); and Alf Hardelin, *The Tractarian Understanding of the Eucharist* (Uppsala: Almquist and Wiksells, 1965).

13. For further discussion of these two interpretations of Eucharistic doctrine, see Nockles, *The Oxford Movement in Context,* 235–48.

Blood of Christ'" (267). In *Annus Domini*, she reminds her readers that receiving the consecrated bread and wine could actually "cleanse" the soul (319). In *The Face of the Deep*, she includes receiving Holy Communion in her list of actions that will help one "overcome Satan and his crew" (326). Furthermore, the receiving of Holy Communion was for Rossetti a profound experience of divine love: "Lord Jesus, evermore give us this Bread, give us Thyself. Thou Who in love givest Thyself to us in the Blessed Sacrament of Thy Body and Blood, grant us grace in love to receive Thee, in love to retain Thee, in love to be joined to Thee eternally" (*FD*, 544). Receiving Holy Communion not only brought Christ within the human soul but also prefigured the final uniting of the soul with Christ in heaven. Rossetti's poem "After Communion," in which the communicant imagines him/herself as St. John at the Last Supper, concludes with thoughts of the final consummation in heaven:

> Now Thou dost bid me come and sup with Thee,
> Now Thou dost make me lean upon Thy breast:
> How will it be with me in time of love?

(CP, 1:229)

When viewed within the context of such beliefs, the Eucharistic scene between Lizzie and Laura, though certainly a scene of love, does not appear as an affirmation of female sensuality or sexuality but rather as an affirmation of the power of the spiritual over the sensual. Indeed, so spiritually meaningful was the receiving of Holy Communion for Rossetti, it is hard to believe that she ever would have used Eucharistic language to represent the power of sensual desires or appetites.

Lizzie's cry of "Eat me, drink me, love me" is summoning not Laura's body but her soul. When Laura kisses Lizzie, she is motivated not by a desire for the goblin fruit but by concern for her sister:

> Lizzie, Lizzie, have you tasted
> For my sake the fruit forbidden?
> Must your light like mine be hidden,
> Your young life like mine be wasted,
> Undone in mine undoing?

(1:23)

In *The Face of the Deep* Rossetti writes, "Love from without can not accomplish its own work unless there is some response from love within" (273). Laura's cry is a sign of love from within. Thus the juices of the goblin fruit work, in a sense, as Rossetti believed the Eucharist did; that is, they cleanse Laura's soul and return her to spiritual health:

> Swift fire spread thro' her veins, knocked at her heart,
> Met the fire smouldering there
> And overbore its lesser flame.

(CP, 1:24)

For Rossetti, fire was "one of the chief symbols of the Divine Presence" (*SF*, 206). Not surprisingly, the stanza describing Laura's renewal begins with reference to the central Christian belief: "Life out of death" (*CP*, 1:25). After a night of anxious watching on Lizzie's part, Laura awakes, returned to her youthful and healthy self, a clear indication that the harmful affects of the goblin fruit have been overcome by divine love.

Rossetti signals this return to spiritual health by indicating that Laura has regained control over her body. She no longer writhes like "one possessed," nor does she kiss Lizzie with a "hungry mouth." Rather, she hugs Lizzie only once, "not twice or thrice." At this point, it is helpful to consider Rossetti's attitude toward the human body in more detail, for in arguing for a reading of the passionate scene between Lizzie and Laura as a scene of sacred rather than erotic love, I am not claiming that Rossetti sees the body and its instincts in entirely negative terms. Certainly, though she was always suspicious of the senses and believed that bodily desires needed to be disciplined, she did not reject the body; in other words, she did not see it as evil.

First, it is instructive to recognize that Rossetti fully embraced the belief in the Incarnation: "Yet as it is by God's appointment that we have our treasure in earthen vessels (2 Cor. 4:7) we become sure that an earthen vessel is suited to the custody of a heavenly treasure: how should it not be, when it pleased God the Son to be partaker of flesh and blood?" (*SF*, 250). Second, Rossetti believed, as a devout Anglican, that at baptism one became, in the words of St. Paul, a "temple of the Holy Ghost." This did not mean she saw the body as a meaningless container but rather that the body, along with the soul, could serve God. In a significant passage in *The Face of the Deep*, when discussing the "burden" of the body, Rossetti writes, "Let not the thing formed say to Him that formed it, Why hast Thou made me thus?—It pleased Christ to redeem us whole, whence we know that our whole being is capable of serving God acceptably. Our body, our soul, our spirit, all are His and endowed for His service" (184).

When Laura gave her body to consumption of goblin fruit, she turned it from God's service. Her sister's Christlike love helped bring her back to spiritual health and thus back to being able to use her body to serve God. When Laura was still yearning for goblin fruit, she could not work; she could not complete any of her physical duties, such as cleaning, milking, or making bread. Returned to spiritual health, she can apparently do all these chores and more, for in the final scene Laura is portrayed as a loving mother with the "little ones" gathered about her. Moreover, she has now assumed the important maternal duty of interpreting for the children the lesson they are to learn from the story of the goblin glen:

> "For there is no friend like a sister
> In calm or stormy weather;
> To cheer one on the tedious way,
> To fetch one if one goes astray,
> To lift one if one totters down,
> To strengthen whilst one stands."
>
> (*CP*, 1:26)

Many twentieth-century readers, especially those who see the poem as an affirmation of woman's sensuality, find this ending problematic. By ending, I am here referring to both the fact of Laura's loving motherhood and the nurserylike poem quoted above, which she offers the children and with which "Goblin Market" concludes. For some, such an ending is a sentimental affirmation of the Victorian values that keep women from the goblin glen and confine them to the home.[14] Others argue that Rossetti does not quite mean what she writes and that "Goblin Market"

14. For example, see Sandra M. Gilbert and Susan Gubar, *The Madwoman in the Attic: The Woman Writer and the Nineteenth-Century Literary Imagination* (New Haven: Yale University Press, 1979), 567, 573.

triumphs over its moral ending by assuring its readers that women do have a right to buy goblin fruit.[15] However, if "Goblin Market" is not just about a woman's body but about the soul and body, then Laura's motherhood and her concluding song are entirely appropriate.

First, by giving Laura the traditional happy ending of marriage and motherhood, Rossetti is able to underscore the saving power of Lizzie's redemptive love. Although the children's stories and fairy tales popular in the nineteenth century often end with moral lessons, in general they do not allow the girl who erred, now grown into motherhood, to offer that lesson. For example, in Perrault's version of "Little Red Riding Hood," not only does the little girl who listened to the wolf not offer the concluding moral, but she also does not live to tell the tale; no kind woodsman rescues her from the wolf's stomach. And while Snow White, from the tales of the Grimm brothers, is revived when the bite of apple is accidentally dislodged from her throat, her story ends with marriage to her prince; she is not portrayed as a wise mother warning others of poison apples.[16]

Second, and most important, Laura's lesson mirrors what Rossetti as the author of "Goblin Market," has done throughout the poem: Laura's song recognizes female sensuality and celebrates woman's spirituality. Lizzie's role—"to cheer," "to fetch," and "to lift"—is, after all, dependent on there being someone who goes astray and totters down. Laura is in a sense warning the "little ones" that as they journey on the "tedious way," they well might eat goblin fruit. However, in making Lizzie, not the goblins or their fruit, the central figure in this song, Laura affirms a woman's spiritual power not only to resist sensual temptations but also to help those who have not been able to do so. Laura's jingle, which asserts, "There is no friend like a sister," replaces the goblin cry "come buy, come buy," which began the poem. Human love that mirrors Christ will triumph over any temptation to place the things of the world before God.

In Laura's song there is an echo of the biblical texts that speak of

15. Jeanie Watson, "'Men Sell Not Such in Any Town': Christina Rossetti's Goblin Fruit of Fairy Tale," *Children's Literature* 12 (1984): 75.

16. For information on Rossetti's childhood reading, see Jan Marsh, *Christina Rossetti: A Writer's Life* (London: Jonathan Cape, 1994), 26. According to Marsh, the fairy tales of Charles Perrault were a "family passion." It is also quite likely that Rossetti was familiar with the Grimm collection of fairy tales as well.

Christ seeking his lost sheep and of Christ laying down his life for his friends. Furthermore, although these last lines of Laura's advice have a certain nursery-like quality, which is, after all, appropriate to an audience of "little ones," they also recall in both form and content the Wisdom literature of Proverbs and the apocryphal Ecclesiasticus.[17] The echoes of Eccles. 6:11–16 are especially striking: "A friend as he continue steadfast, shall be to thee as thyself. . . . A faithful friend is a strong defence: and he that hath found him hath found a treasure. Nothing can be compared to a faithful friend, and no weight of gold and silver is able to countervail the goodness of his fidelity. A faithful friend is the medicine of life and immortality: and they that fear the Lord shall find him." Thus Rossetti not only associates Laura with the wise, experienced masculine voices of these Old Testament texts but also shifts the emphasis from the masculine to the feminine. Instead of having a wise man of the world speak to a "son," as is the pattern in both Proverbs and Ecclesiasticus, Rossetti offers in the form of a Christian fairy tale an experienced woman speaking to daughters. (Rossetti does not specify the sex of the children, but readers typically see them as female.) Just as Rossetti replaced the expected masculine savior with a female savior, she concludes by replacing the expected masculine voice with a feminine one and, moreover, a feminine voice that speaks of sisterhood and female friendship in the elevated terms used in the Bible to speak of masculine friendship.

In drawing attention to these reversals in gender expectations, I am not suggesting that "Goblin Market" should be read as a utopian text in which a corrupt patriarchal society is replaced by a pure matriarchal society. Such an interpretation, as we shall see from Rossetti's position on the woman question, would associate her with a feminist political view that she did not espouse. I am claiming, however, that in the Lizzie and Laura relationship, Rossetti offers her audience two lessons pertaining to women and the life of the soul, which for Victorian England in the 1860s might well be seen as subversive. First, through Lizzie, Rossetti indicates that the self-sacrificing love Victorian women were to embody should not be seen as angelic but as Christlike; in other words, she indicates that

17. Marshall suggests that Rossetti's "there is no friend like a sister" is perhaps intended to be read as a supplement to Prov. 18:24: "There is a friend that sticketh closer than a brother" (439).

women were capable of a higher level of spiritual existence and action than that of ministering angel in the home. One might also infer that a woman need not be a wife to fulfill that spiritual potential, for when Lizzie won the "fiery antidote" for sin, she was a sister who was not yet wife and mother. Second, by celebrating sisterhood, Rossetti reminds her readers that the religious concept of brotherly love spoken of in the Bible should be seen to encompass sisterly love as well. Significantly, the last image is not even of mother and children, but of two sisters, one helping the other on the "tedious way."

Critical interpretation of "The Prince's Progress" focuses on the prince's failure to make spiritual progress on his tedious way. (Interestingly, "tedious" is a key word, used by Rossetti three times to describe particular moments in the prince's quest.) Noting the echoes of Bunyan's *Pilgrim's Progress*, scholars have concluded that Rossetti is offering a reversal of that allegory. Instead of overcoming temptation and reaching the Celestial City, as the good pilgrim does, Rossetti's wayward prince succumbs to every temptation that comes his way and arrives "too late." When he arrives at the promised land of "wine, oil, and bread," his princess, seen by most critics as emblematic of his soul or Heaven itself, is dead. Thus, rather than save his soul, as Bunyan's Christian does, Rossetti's indolent prince loses it.[18]

As this summary indicates, the standard interpretation of the poem focuses on the prince. He is, after all, the title character, and certainly Rossetti intends his failure to be read as a warning about the need to prepare one's soul for the Last Judgment. Indeed, in the 1875 edition, by positioning "The Prince's Progress" immediately after "Goblin Market," Rossetti underscores the prince's spiritual failure. Reading "The Prince's Progress" as a sequel to "Goblin Market," we see the prince as Lizzie's opposite. He is easily led astray by the milkmaid; he continually finds the way "tedious"; and when he is tested by the raging floods, he cannot even keep himself standing, let alone help another. Not surprisingly, when he arrives with what he believes is an elixir of life, he is too late,

---

18. For two excellent articles that develop a reading of the prince's failure within a Christian framework, see Joan Rees, "Christina Rossetti: Poet," *Critical Quarterly* 26 (1984): 59–72; and Mary Arseneau, "Pilgrimage and Postponement: Christina Rossetti's 'The Prince's Progress,'" *Victorian Poetry* 32 (autumn–winter 1994): 277–98.

whereas Lizzie saves Laura from death by bringing her the "fiery antidote" in time. Such a comparison between these two poems, however, raises questions about the role of the princess.[19] Are we to compare her to Lizzie or Laura? And what does Rossetti suggest regarding the princess when she positions "The Prince's Progress" as a sequel to "Goblin Market"?

On one level, the princess appears an admirable character, a woman who fulfills her prescribed role by waiting patiently for her prince. Compared to Lizzie, however, she seems decidedly unheroic, and her passivity becomes problematic. Are we then to see her as Laura? She wastes away as Laura did when she ate the goblin fruit, and she dies, as Laura would have, had Lizzie not acted. If the princess resembles Laura, then what is the nature of her sin? In posing such questions, I am not suggesting that a reading focusing on the princess entirely replace one focusing on the prince, but rather that we recognize the multiple levels of this poem. In this long narrative poem telling of a princely failure is a subplot involving the princess' progress or, more appropriately, her lack of progress, as well. "The Prince's Progress" offers not one but two cautionary tales. The second, that of the sleeping princess, is especially appropriate for Victorian women who had been taught that marriage would awaken them to love.

The female chorus in the poem, presumably those women who are the handmaidens to the princess, describe her as "spell-bound." This female chorus does not elaborate on the nature of this spell. For example, they do not tell us who cast the spell or why. All we can conclude from their admonitions to the prince is that the princess is confined to her "white room" to wait for him to come to her. However, unlike the folktale Sleeping Beauty, which the princess' story so strongly echoes, this spell does not hold time still. Whereas the princess of the fairy tale sleeps an ageless sleep for one hundred years and awakes still beautiful just as the timely prince appears in her chamber or, as in some versions, just as he kisses her, Rossetti's princess grows old; and apparently, just before her not-so-timely prince arrives, she dies. The dirge for the dead princess that

19. Dawn Henwood is one of the few critics who question the role of the princess; see "Christian Allegory and Subversive Poetics: Christina Rossetti's *Prince's Progress* Reexamined," *Victorian Poetry* 35 (spring 1997): 83–94.

84

concludes "The Prince's Progress" is indeed what Rossetti herself referred to as a "reverse of the *Sleeping Beauty*."[20]

The handmaidens hold the prince entirely responsible for the fact that the happy ending of the Sleeping Beauty tale does not become a reality for their princess:

"Too late for love, too late for joy,
  Too late, too late!
You loitered on the road too long,
  You trifled at the gate:
The enchanted dove upon her branch
  Died without a mate;
The enchanted princess in her tower
  Slept, died, behind the grate;
Her heart was starving all this while
  You made it wait."

(*CP*, 1:108)

This prince is guilty of sloth and, as Mary Arseneau convincingly notes, of repeatedly misreading the spiritual significance of his quest.[21] But, is he responsible for the princess never having known joy? Is the reader to accept without question the judgment of these handmaidens?

When the princess "weepeth" and asks how long she must wait, her handmaidens reply, "Till the strong Prince comes, who must come in time . . . Sleep, dream and sleep" (*CP*, 1:95). In other words, they respond by offering her the story of Sleeping Beauty. And although they indicate that there is "a mountain to climb" and a "river to ford," they nevertheless encourage the princess to believe that the prince shall triumph over these obstacles. They have even "muffled the chime" so that she might sleep and thus ignore the passage of time. It is noteworthy that an amused ironic narrative voice undercuts the voices of these women by introducing this "strong Prince" as "taking his ease on cushion and mat" (1:95). The reader is thus encouraged from the very beginning of

20. Christina G. Rossetti to Dora Greenwell, [October 1863], *The Collected Letters of Christina Rossetti*, ed. Antony H. Harrison, 4 vols. (Charlottesville: University Press of Virginia, 1997), 1:184.
21. Arseneau, "Pilgrimage and Postponement," 280.

the poem to recognize that the prince will fail and that there will be no happy marriage ending for the princess. However, the female chorus, though it berates the prince and occasionally warns him of his "doom," never urges the princess to action. "Better dream than weep" is the essence of their advice. Furthermore, the princess appears to accept such advice, never seeming to consider the possibility that the prince might fail. Sleeping and dreaming, though the proper role of the fairy-tale princess, is, within Rossetti's reverse Sleeping Beauty, a more questionable activity.

As critics have noted, Rossetti employs the nuptial imagery of both Matt. 25:1–10 and the Song of Songs throughout the poem.[22] However, I would argue that this princess does not prove to be either a wise virgin who keeps her lamp lit waiting to greet the bridegroom or the bride of the Song of Songs who so yearns for her lover that she "seeks" him and "will not let him go" (Song of Songs 3:1–4). One need only recall Rossetti's convent poems, such as "Three Nuns" or "An 'Immurata' Sister," to see that this princess is not actively preparing her soul to meet Christ the Bridegroom. Especially striking is the contrast between this sleeping princess and Rossetti's description, in *The Face of the Deep*, of the church as Christ's bride coming to meet him on the Last Day:

> She comes forth from the thousand battle-fields of the fierce fight of her afflictions. Beds of weariness, haunts of starvation, hospital wards, rescue homes, orphanages, leper colonies, fires of martyrdom, in these and such as these did she set up mirrors whereby to fashion herself after Christ's likeness. . . . Every gift, every grace, arrays and adorns her; innocence, penitence, purity, purification, largeness of heart as the sand of the sea; weighty judgment, mercy, faith; carefulness in well doing, as mint and anise and cummin; no longer patience yet fruits of patience; no longer chastening, yet its peaceable fruit of righteousness; hope that maketh not ashamed, love superseding all that is not love or love's. She has forgotten her own people and her father's house, has forgotten all who are not of her or with her, in the supreme moment of going home to Him Whom her soul loveth. She has come up from the wilderness lean-

22. For example, see ibid.

ing upon her Beloved, and leaning upon Him she will sit down in the Promised Land flowing with milk and honey. (436)

When we compare the passive princess of "The Prince's Progress" to this powerful description of Christ's bride, the princess pales. Rossetti has written not only a reverse Sleeping Beauty but also a reverse Song of Songs. Thus there can be no springtime ending for the princess, no awakening from her deathlike sleep.

Although death need not be read as a sign of spiritual failure, Rossetti does create a scene that is decidedly unsettling in terms of the Christian framework of the poem. The princess' attendants suggest that perhaps she has found in death if not joy, at least peace, when they ask, "Or is the hunger fed at length / Cast off the care?" (*CP*, 1:109). Yet Rossetti leaves this central question unanswered. Moreover, the flower imagery offers little comfort. As the princess slept, lilies and rosebuds grew by her head, and red and white poppies grew at her feet. Only the white poppies, symbolic of the sleep of death, appear in this final scene as appropriate for her. Perhaps understandably, the handmaidens refuse the red roses, symbolic of love, which the prince brings: "Let be these poppies that we strew, / Your roses are too red" (1:110). One might also accept the absence of the red poppies as appropriate, for according to some versions of flower lore, red poppies are symbolic of consolation.[23] Certainly, neither princess nor prince is being consoled. However, most troubling is the absence of the lilies, which Christian tradition has long associated with purity and faith. Rossetti herself found the lily especially emblematic of religious faith. Inside a presentation copy of *Verses*, her collection of religious poetry, she wrote, "Faith is like a lily, lifted high and white."[24]

I would not argue that the princess is a lost soul, damned with her prince, but her death is certainly a cautionary sign. The princess waited for a marriage to a "strong Prince," a fantasy creature of romance who did not exist, and as a result, her spiritual life was stunted. Instead of patterning herself after the bride in the Song of Songs, the princess imagined herself to be the sleeping beauty of the fairy tale. Furthermore, if we con-

---

23. See Beverly Seaton, *The Language of Flowers: A History* (Charlottesville: University Press of Virginia, 1995), 188–89.

24. Mackenzie Bell, "Christina Rossetti," *Author* (March 1895): 269.

sider "The Prince's Progress" in comparison to "Goblin Market," we notice that although sympathetic, the women surrounding the princess did not tell stories that would encourage her to love, to help a sister on the "tedious way," as Laura does at the end of "Goblin Market." And if we consider "Maiden-Song" as the sequel to the story of the sleeping princess, then we find in Margaret the princess' opposite. When we read "The Prince's Progress" as framed by these two other fairy-tale poems, then we see that the female community, represented by the handmaidens, and the princess herself must bear some of the responsibility for her story ending not with marriage but death.

Although both the princess and Margaret are portrayed by Rossetti as women who wait, Margaret, in contrast, the "fairest" of the three sisters, is not waiting for love or marriage. She is a fairy-tale heroine, but unlike the sleeping princess, she is not controlled by the plot of such tales. One might see Margaret as a Cinderella who does not appear interested in going to the ball. When her two envious sisters, Meggan and May, wander off to find strawberry leaves, for "strawberry leaves and May-dew / Make maidens fair" (*CP*, 1:111), Margaret stays home to sing and sew, and she is apparently content to do so. Only when she is worried about her sisters does she look out the door. When she hears "a distant nightingale," she goes as far as the garden gate, but again, she is waiting for her sisters, not a fantasy lover. Moreover, when she sings her song, it is not to attract a husband, as the songs of her sisters have done, but rather she sings to answer the nightingale's complaint:

> Waiting thus in weariness
>    She marked the nightingale
> Telling, if any one would heed,
>    Its old complaining tale.
> Then lifted she her voice and sang,
>    Answering the bird:
> Then lifted she her voice and sang,
>    Such notes were never heard
> From any bird where Spring's in blow.

(1:115)

Her love song is an answer to desire and longing. Margaret is the figure of love the sleeping princess should have been. Margaret does not wait for love; rather, she loves.

Significantly, her song unites and harmonizes all: "Every beast and bird and fish / Came mustering to the sound" (1:115). Even her wandering sisters return home. Indeed, all humanity is attracted to Margaret's song. Not only does the king of "all that country" respond, but apparently all his subjects as well:

> No foot too feeble for the ascent,
>     Not any head too grey;
> Some were swift and none were slow.
>
> (1:116)

Her song not only overcomes the envy of her sisters, but as she sings to her king, she also brings "together friend and foe" (1:116). Unlike the waiting princess in "The Prince's Progress" but resembling Lizzie in "Goblin Market," Margaret can be seen as an embodiment of human love that mirrors divine love. Hence, when Margaret is first described, she is associated with both flag flowers (also called iris), which Lizzie also picks in "Goblin Market," and red poppies, which were so noticeably absent from the bier of the dead princess:

> But when Margaret plucked a flag-flower,
>     Or poppy hot aflame,
> All the beasts and all the birds
>     And all the fishes came
> To her hand more soft than snow.
>
> (1:110)

In Christian art, irises often appear as emblems of both the Virgin Mary and Christ. The red poppy not only symbolizes consolation but in Christian tradition is also associated with Christ's Passion. Also relevant is the legend of St. Margaret, a version of which tells of the poppy getting its red color from the blood of the dragon "slain by holy Maid Margaret."[25] Rossetti rewards Margaret with the most prestigious marriage of the three sisters because she is the "fairest" not just physically but spiritually

---

25. Charles M. Skinner, *Myths and Legends of Flowers, Trees, Fruits, and Plants* (Philadelphia: Lippincott, 1911), 140–41, 227.

as well, and her spirituality shows itself in the love she engenders in other creatures, both animal and human.

Although Meggan and May have the power to attract others, their power has a sinister quality. When Meggan and May sing, their suitors respond as if enchanted, in other words, as if they have lost control. For example, May's shepherd forgets his duty to his flocks, "His panting flocks, / In parching hill-side drouth" (*CP*, 1:113). In creating Margaret's envious sisters, Rossetti has not only drawn upon the evil stepsisters of fairy-tale lore but also on the figure of the femme fatale. Though the sisters do not destroy their lovers, they think only of themselves in marrying, not of the men who kneel before them. When Meggan's herdsman proposes, she muses:

> "Better be first with him,
> Than dwell where fairer Margaret sits,
> Who shines my brightness dim."
>
> (1:113)

May responds in a similar manner: "Where Margaret shines like the sun / I shine but like a moon." A desire for power and position is their motivation for marrying, not love. Meggan muses: "I shall be lady of his love, / And he shall worship me." For Meggan and May, marriage is merely a social arrangement, one that allows them to escape comparison with Margaret and thus gain power. In Margaret's case, however, marriage can be seen not only in social terms but in religious terms as well.

First, Margaret engages in no such questionable musing. Furthermore, when she finished her song, the king, who had been kneeling at her feet, simply "stood up like a royal man / And claimed her for his bride" (1:116). He has recognized her "maiden majesty," but unlike his weaker counterparts, herdsman and shepherd, he has not been under any spell cast by her song. Second, and most important, Margaret and her king invite recollections of the celestial marriage, that is, the marriage of the church and Christ. Such similarities become especially apparent when one reads "Maiden-Song" with certain of Rossetti's devotional poems in mind. For example, the final scene of "Maiden-Song" resembles the concluding lines of Rossetti's " 'The Holy City, New Jerusalem,' " a poem describing the triumphant entry of the redeemed into heaven after the Second Coming of Christ:

> God bring us to Jerusalem,
>     God bring us home in peace;
> The strong who stand, the weak who fall,
> The first and last, the great and small,
> Home one by one, home one and all.

(CP, 2:280)

Especially striking are the similarities between Margaret and Rossetti's descriptions of Christ's bride, the church. For example, the second stanza of "'She Shall Be Brought unto the King'" recalls the power of Margaret's song of love:

> Perfect her notes in the perfect harmonies;
> With tears wiped away, no conscience of sin,
>     Loss forgotten and sorrowful memories.

(2:281)

And the description of the bride in "Who is this that cometh up not alone" recalls Margaret's "maiden majesty":

> Lo, the King of kings' daughter, a high princess,
> Going home as bride to her Husband's Throne,
>     Virgin queen in perfected loveliness.

(2:282)

Appropriately, Rossetti concludes this series of three Christian fairy tales with a marriage that can be read as emblematic of that between Christ and the church triumphant.

In *Time Flies,* Rossetti devotes three consecutive entries to a meditation on human love, in which she finds, in the forget-me-not and a sea-shell, emblems of love. Her concluding remarks might well serve as a gloss for these three poems:

> Our study of a forget-me-not and of a shell will not entail loss of time—that irreparable loss!—if it helps us to realize that all recip-

rocal human love worthy of the name, exhibits a tinge of heaven as well as a warmth and colouring of earth.

That it is so far selfless as to be only one harmonious part of a better whole.

That it is faithful, fitting into nothing except its own other self.

And that unless it sets Christ before us at least as in a glass darkly, it were good for it not to have been born. (132)

The love of Lizzie and Laura sets Christ before the reader as does the love of Margaret for her wandering sisters and her king. The sleeping princess never learned this lesson on how to give love "worthy of the name."

Rossetti's dissatisfaction with Victorian marriage and her cynical views of romantic love most likely arose from a variety of reasons. As discussed in Chapter 2, the movement to reestablish the consecrated religious life within the Church of England played a role. And as Sharon Leder and Andrea Abbott argue, the various political movements of the 1850s and the 1860s to enlarge a woman's rights within marriage might have influenced her thoughts as well.[26] Perhaps during these years, even Rossetti's situation as an unmarried woman and her personal observations of those involved in married life contributed to some of her conclusions. Quite possibly, she viewed with questioning eyes the vision of love at times portrayed in Dante Gabriel Rossetti's paintings. Yet, by the time Rossetti wrote "Maiden-Song," she was willing to celebrate marriage and married love as long as the marriage celebrated was not merely a social arrangement but a religious union as well.

Moreover, as both "Goblin Market" and "Maiden-Song" indicate, Rossetti wrote poems that depict the healing power of human love. Thus, to label Rossetti as antimarriage or to argue that she always depicted human love as false is to misrepresent her position on human love. Furthermore, seeing Rossetti only as a poet of betrayed love might lead to the conclusion that she saw women only as victims of their society and not as individuals who had the power to heal a society and to create community, as Lizzie and Margaret do. Although Rossetti certainly

26. Sharon Leder with Andrea Abbott, *The Language of Exclusion: The Poetry of Emily Dickinson and Christina Rossetti* (Westport, Conn.: Greenwood Press, 1987), 120–32.

might have experienced moments when she viewed woman as the hopeless and powerless victim, it is significant that in 1875 she chose to frame the poem of the passive princess with poems that depict woman not as waiting for love but as giving love.

*four*

# THE FALLEN WOMAN POEMS

☦

ONE OF THE RECURRING FIGURES IN BOTH VICTORIAN ART AND
literature is that of the fallen woman, the woman who has had sexual in-
tercourse outside of marriage and who therefore is isolated from the
community, in a sense cut off from human love, for what is seen as both
sin and social crime. The four ballads—"Light Love" (1856), "An Apple-
Gathering" (1857), "Cousin Kate" (1859), "Margery" (1863)—and the
monologue "'The Iniquity of the Fathers Upon the Children'" (1865),
all tell this woman's story. "Light Love," "Cousin Kate," and "'The Iniquity of the Fathers '" all include the presence of an illegitimate child,
and thus the sexual nature of the woman's fall is made explicit. In "An
Apple-Gathering," the imagery of picked blossoms and the fact that the
speaker must "loiter," apparently homeless as night falls, both suggest that
she is a fallen woman. In "Margery," the narrator's description of Margery as "shamefaced" and the comment that she has made herself
"cheap" signify her fallen state in the eyes of her neighbors. Rossetti was
most likely first introduced to this outcast figure through the literature
she read as a young woman. Percy's *Reliques,* one of the books popular
in the Rossetti family, contains several folk ballads of the seduced and
abandoned woman, and several of Rossetti's immediate predecessors,
such as Elizabeth Barrett Browning, Caroline Norton, and William
Wordsworth, all wrote poems focusing on such an outcast figure. More-

over, by the 1850s, while Rossetti was writing her own variations on the fallen woman's story, both prostitution, commonly referred to as the Great Social Evil, and illegitimacy had become major topics of concern for Victorian society in general and for the religious community in particular. By 1859, Rossetti herself, strongly influenced by her faith, had become directly involved in the cause to save fallen women by assisting in the work of the London Diocesan Penitentiary, one of the many houses of mercy established during these years to reclaim the fallen.

Considering Rossetti's fallen woman poems in both their literary and social contexts indicates that Rossetti, unlike many of her contemporaries, saw the fallen woman's story as a complex and layered narrative, one in which the fallen woman was not the only sinner. In these fallen woman ballads, as Rossetti begins to turn the reader's eyes from the fallen woman to others who played a role in her story, even her counterpart, the pure bride, is implicated. For Rossetti, the fallen woman is guilty, but her guilt must be shared.

"Light Love," completed in October 1856, is the first of Rossetti's fallen women ballads. Upon first reading, this ballad appears to follow the typical scenario of seduction and betrayal. In fact, "Light Love" does recall a particular scene in Caroline Norton's "Sorrows of Rosalie" in which Lord Arthur cruelly dismisses Rosalie and their illegitimate child while his bride-to-be waits nearby. A close consideration reveals, however, that Rossetti has written not so much a seduced woman's lament as a lovers' argument. In so doing, she draws significant attention to the man's role, so that by the end of the poem it is evident that the title applies more to the man than the woman. In other words, the one for whom the love was "light," frivolous, and of small importance, is the male speaker.

Significantly, Rossetti begins the poem with his voice:

> "Oh sad thy lot before I came,
>   But sadder when I go;
> My presence but a flash of flame,
>   A transitory glow
>   Between two barren wastes like snow."

(CP, 1:136)

These images of waste and barrenness recall several earlier, nineteenth-century fallen woman poems. Typically, however, it is more common for the fallen woman herself to speak of her wasted life, as in Norton's "Sorrows of Rosalie," or Elizabeth Barrett Browning's "A Year's Spinning," or to have some sympathetic narrator do so, as in Coventry Patmore's "The Woodman's Daughter" and William Wordsworth's "The Thorn." By having the man who has in a sense made the woman's life a wasteland actually use such imagery, Rossetti underscores his arrogance and heartlessness. Although he associates his "presence" in her life with heat, he is in fact cold.

When the woman herself does speak, her words first seem in keeping with the traditional seduced and pining female, for she speaks of warming herself with the memories of her lover, thus indicating she still loves despite his betrayal. Yet Rossetti appears to introduce this convention into the poem only later to have her female speaker discard it. After the man suggests the woman find some other "love / Left from the days of old" to provide for her, she recognizes the emptiness of his love: "Even let it go, the love that harms." She then turns to her child: "We twain will never part" (*CP*, 1:138). She admits that the man's love was "light" and contrasts it with the more enduring qualities of maternal love.

The narrative descriptions of the mother holding and kissing the baby ("She hushed the baby at her breast, / She rocked it on her knee") can be read as signs of a genuine love for the child; yet the man interprets her comment and gestures as a taunt, for he then delivers another verbal blow:

"Now never teaze me, tender-eyed,
　Sigh-voiced," he said in scorn:
"For nigh at hand there blooms a bride,
　My bride before the morn;
　Ripe-blooming she, as thou forlorn.
Ripe-blooming she, my rose, my peach;
　She wooes me day and night:
I watch her tremble in my reach;
　She reddens, my delight;
　She ripens, reddens in my sight."

(*CP*, 1:137–38)

His implication appears to be that although this "forlorn" woman may have this child to keep, he will soon marry a "rose," "a peach," and produce other children.

This mention of the blooming bride, the supposed opposite of the fallen woman, leads to another unexpected turn. Often in folk ballads and their literary imitations, a vast difference between fallen woman and virgin is either implied or stated; however, Rossetti blurs these distinctions considerably. First, she has the female speaker compare her own outcast state to this bride by imagining that she too will some day be cast aside: "Alas for her, poor faded rose, / Alas for her, like me." This prediction motivates the man to deliver his final blow: "Like thee? nay not like thee: / She leans, but from a guarded tree" (1:138). Although his bride-to-be woos him, she has not had sexual relations with him, and thus the male speaker insists that his blooming bride-to-be is the opposite of his rejected lover. Yet Rossetti calls into question his claim that the two women differ by having him use sexual imagery to describe his bride.

As the imagery of ripening fruit and flowers implies, the man sees his bride primarily in sexual terms, and thus despite his denial of any similarity between the "forlorn" woman and this ripening "peach," the similarity remains. In both cases, the woman is for him a sexual object, and the only difference between the unwed mother and the bride is embodied in the image of the "guarded tree." His "peach" is so carefully guarded that marriage is the only way he can gain access to her. Whether she is responsible for such restraint or whether she is guarded by others is not clear; however, what is clear, is that ironically, her inaccessibility increases both her worth and her current sexual appeal in the male speaker's eyes.

The implication that a woman's most valuable possession is her virginity, and therefore she must be certain to exchange it only for marriage, lies behind this metaphor of fruit and guarded tree. In this implication Rossetti follows the typical patterns. For example, in such folk ballads as "The Lady's Fall" and "Lady Anne Bothwell's Lament," both included in Percy's *Reliques,* such a warning is explicitly delivered from the fallen woman to the imagined maidens reading the text. Furthermore, the literary ballads previously mentioned—Wordsworth's "The Thorn," Patmore's "The Woodman's Daughter," and Browning's "A Year's Spinning"— offer a similar warning in that in each, the abandoned woman either goes mad, dies, or is dying. Thus all these poems warn the female reader that illicit love brings only madness or death, not marriage.

Although Rossetti's ballad also conveys the message that men will not marry fallen women, by having such views revealed directly through the male speaker's words, she casts a shadow over the subjects of both romantic love and marriage. Even though the male speaker participated in devaluing another woman's worth by seducing her, he still places such a high price on virginity that he is willing to buy it with marriage. Such a transaction suggests that the bride and fallen woman are indeed similar; both, in a sense, must sell themselves. Thus, love appears to have little to do with either the man's past love affair or his coming marriage. In fact, the title might be seen at this point as referring not just to the small importance of the love he offers but to the fallen nature of that love.

"Light" was an adjective still used in the nineteenth century as referring to a wanton or unchaste person, especially a woman.[1] Significantly, however, Rossetti not only changes the expected gender in that the man appears guiltier of unchaste love than the unwed mother, but she also gives the words "true love" to the fallen woman: "Thou leavest love, true love behind." The man's sin is not just the seduction of this woman but the betrayal of love itself through his promiscuous behavior. And by the end of the poem, he appears more the sinner than she, for Rossetti concludes the poem with judgment focused on the man, not the woman: "She raised her eyes, not wet / But hard, to Heaven: 'Does God forget?'" (*CP*, 1:138). This question has an implied answer, especially for someone sharing Rossetti's religious beliefs: no, God does not forget. This fallen woman's story is unfinished and will be brought to a conclusion only when this man, this "light love," faces her again at the Last Judgment, a time when Rossetti believed, as did many of her faith, that everyone would have to face those we had harmed on earth. In her later devotional work *The Face of the Deep*, she writes, "I myself must face on that Day and at the Bar all whom I have ever affected on earth, all who directly or remotely have responded to my influence for good or evil" (70). Thus, Rossetti's poem is not just a poem to warn young women to beware of deceiving men, but a warning to the deceivers themselves. The final image of the fallen woman, holding her baby, looking up to

---

1. See, for example, Robert Browning's "Light Love."

heaven with "hard" eyes does not so much evoke pity, as so many nineteenth-century depictions of the fallen women do, as it evokes fear of judgment and retribution for those who have in some way contributed to such a woman's fall.

I do not mean to imply that such harsh judgment of the man involved in the woman's fall is without precedent. For example, the Scottish ballad "The Ruined Maid's Lament," a ballad Rossetti might have read in her copy of Robert Burns, concludes with a warning delivered from the narrator: "but Heaven's curse will blast the man / Denies the bairn he got." And certainly any sympathetic portrayal of the fallen woman, such as Browning's "A Year's Spinning" or Patmore's "Woodman's Daughter," casts negative light upon the man who seduced her. I do wish, however, to point out that it is characteristic of Rossetti's treatment of the subject of illicit love to underscore the fact that in every fallen woman's story there is a guilty man. While "Light Love" provides the most striking example of Rossetti's fallen man, her subsequent ballads continue to draw the reader's attention to the man's role in the woman's fall. In "An Apple-Gathering," although the fallen man does not speak, he is given a name, Willie, and we see evidence of his heartlessness when he walks by with another woman. In "Cousin Kate," the fallen woman begins her story by telling that the lord "lured" her from her cottage home to use her as his "plaything," only later to "change" her "like a glove." "Margery" concludes with the sympathetic narrator denouncing Margery's seducer: "Were I the man she's fretting for / I should my very self abhor" (*CP*, 3:290). In the monologue, "'The Iniquity,'" the illegitimate daughter angrily asks concerning her father, "Why did he set his snare / To catch at unaware / My mother's foolish youth?" (*CP*, 1:178).

While Rossetti's representations of faithless seducers have plenty of literary antecedents, her treatment of the pure woman he marries sets her handling of the subject apart from the one of the dominant literary conventions of the time regarding the representation of woman. It is perhaps a commonplace of scholarship that Victorians contributed to a long tradition of depicting womanhood in dichotomous terms that focused on a woman's sexuality (virgin vs. whore, madonna vs. magdalene), and that the dominant domestic ideal of wife, at least for the middle class, was that of the angel, who was sexually innocent. In her fallen woman poems, Rossetti repeatedly questions the typical distinctions made between fallen and unfallen women by implying that all virgin brides and chaste wives are not necessarily guiltless; for while remaining sexually pure, they have not been without guile. Such questioning of the virgin/bride stereotype is implied in "Light Love," in the man's description of his bride who "leans from a guarded tree" and is more explicitly explored by Rossetti in "Cousin Kate," "Margery," and "Apple-Gathering."

In "Cousin Kate," Kate, who is seen by the neighbors as "good and pure," appears to have sold herself to the lord for money and position:

> O cousin Kate, my love was true,
>     Your love was writ in sand:
> If he had fooled not me but you,
>     If you stood where I stand,
> He'd not have won me with his love
>     Nor bought me with his land.

(CP, 1:32)

Of course, this accusation is made by the angry outcast woman, and we do not hear Cousin Kate's side of the story, but at the very least, Cousin Kate has betrayed her fallen cousin by marrying that cousin's seducer. Kate, the supposedly unfallen woman, appears more corrupt than her fallen cousin in that she was not "fooled"; she knew what she was doing. Rossetti's "Cousin Kate" questions the simplistic terms of feminine purity as defined by her society. The "neighbours" still call Kate "good and pure" only because the lord "bound [her] with a ring." The word "bound" is especially telling, for it associates the image of wife with that of the slave. For a wedding ring, Kate has become the lord's possession.

"Margery" offers a similar critique of woman's role in courtship. The narrator, a sympathetic member of the community, comments on Margery's mistake, which appears to be not so much her sexual fall, but the fact that she did not know the rules of the courtship game:

> A foolish girl, to love a man
>     And let him know she loved him so!
> She should have tried another plan;
>     Have loved, but not have let him know:
>     Then he perhaps had loved her so.

(CP, 3:289)

That Rossetti found society's encouragement of such feminine coyness and guile problematic is especially apparent in "An Apple-Gathering." Rossetti begins the poem with the emphasis on the act that led to the fallen woman's empty-handed state, but an act that appears to have been committed without guile: "I plucked pink blossoms from mine apple tree / And wore them all that evening in my hair" (*CP*, 1:43). Of course, her tree without blossoms will bear no fruit: "that evening," for a momentary happiness, she exchanged future security. In the eyes of the community, she has been foolish: "My neighbours mocked me while they saw me pass / So empty-handed back" (1:43). Clearly, because her tree produced no apples, she will have trouble establishing her own home. Willie has now jilted her for Gertrude, who has a basket full of apples: "Plump Gertrude passed me with her basket full, / A stronger hand than hers helped it along" (1: 44). Because the speaker showed her preference for Willie before the proper season, before marriage, she has lost her potential for a home.

Up to this point in the poem, Rossetti appears to have written the standard warning to female readers to keep virginal until marriage. However, she calls the whole process of Victorian courtship into question with the speaker's plea:

Ah Willie, Willie, was my love less worth
    Than apples with their green leaves piled above?
I counted rosiest apples on the earth
    Of far less worth than love.

(1:44)

This doleful lament is an affirmation of the values that led her to pluck "pink blossoms for her hair." In this stanza the image of the plucked blossom that at first appears to symbolize the woman's foolish impatience and fallen state is presented as a symbol of love. Thus Rossetti suggests that although in the eyes of her neighbors the speaker's love has been foolish, because it has not led to marriage, it was, nevertheless, true. Similarly, the symbolic significance of the apples also changes. The first association of the apples with home and security is now tainted, for apples now symbolize merely a commodity that a woman exchanges for the security of marriage. Because Gertrude has a basket full of apples, she gets Willie's helping hand. Love seems to have little to do with this exchange. More-over, "rosiest apples" can be read as a metaphor for material things of the earth as well, and thus Willie appears to have placed finance before love. In fact, his sin, as seen through the fallen woman's eyes, is not so much the initial seduction as it is the subsequent betrayal of her love. Both Ger-trude and Willie are guilty of participating in a loveless transaction. Thus, while the speaker is still guilty of a sinful love, the others are guilty of placing the things of the earth before love. Rossetti's use of apple imagery of course invites thoughts of a fallen world; however, she has altered the conventional iconography by associating one of the traditional symbols of the Fall not with the fallen woman but with the supposedly pure women. The speaker can gather no apples, whereas Lilias and Lilian and Gertrude have baskets full. While their neighbors might see these women as pure, clearly Rossetti does not.

These four ballads all contain signs that Rossetti was less preoccupied with a woman's virginity as a measure of her goodness than were many of her contemporaries. In these fallen woman poems, Rossetti suggests that there is not much difference between the woman who sells herself for marriage, who thus does not marry for a genuine love, and the woman who has sexual experience before marriage because she is fooled by the promises of romantic love. Both are guilty of placing the things of the earth (whether romantic love or material security) before God. Fur-thermore, in all these poems, the fallen woman remains alive; in other words, Rossetti does not employ the traditional ending by having her die or go mad. As previously mentioned, the woman in "Light Love" looks to heaven for justice and perhaps comfort. The speaker in Cousin Kate may have to "howl in dust," but she is alive and she shows no signs of weakness. Margery is pining and fading but the speaker has plans to save her: "I'll not see / Her blossom fade" (*CP*, 3:290). And although the speaker in "An Apple-Gathering" apparently has no home to shelter her, she is still alive at the end of the poem. In a sense, Rossetti provides no convenient endings, and therefore no comfortable sense of closure is of-fered. The reader is left to imagine what will happen next.

So prevalent was the belief that a fallen woman must die that of course it is possible a Victorian reader would imagine a death ending no matter what Rossetti wrote. Possibly, readers might also have seen these seduced and abandoned women as only one step from prostitution and therefore one step closer to death. A common belief of the time was that seduction was the first step in the downward path toward prostitution. In 1860, for example, one reformer concluded that despite contrary evidence suggesting that the "lowness of wages" drives many women to a life of "infamy and woe," many Victorians still believed that "woman is first betrayed, then deserted, and driven to street prostitution."[2] Many also accepted that a prostitute was doomed to die young.[3] In fact, many believed that at most she would last seven years, for disease or suicide would soon claim her.[4] Often, literature contributed to the existence or at least the prevalence of such beliefs. For example, William Bell Scott's "Rosabell," "Within and Without: A London Lyric" by Barry Cornwall [Bryan Procter], Dora Greenwell's "Christina," Jean Ingelow's "Perdita," Dante Gabriel Rossetti's "Jenny," and Thomas Hood's "Bridge of Sighs" (the most popular "social evil" poem of the period) all remind the reader that the prostitute was once an innocent young woman, and that her fall into prostitution began with the man who first seduced her or, as in "Jenny," began with "man's lust." Furthermore, in all these poems except "Jenny," the prostitute is either dead or dying, and even Dante Gabriel Rossetti's "Jenny" offers little hope she will escape what the speaker sees as her polluted life.

Although Rossetti could not control what her readers imagined for her literary fallen women, her decision to involve herself in the saving of actual fallen women indicates that she at least could imagine another ending for a fallen woman's life's story besides that of an early death. Rossetti's religion would have led her to see an illicit sexual relationship as a sin against purity, but that same religious faith certainly would lead her to see a woman's sexual fall as forgivable. God's love was infinite, even if man's was not: Jesus would not have the "woman taken in adultery" stoned; he simply told her to "Go and sin no more" (John 8:11). This belief in God's mercy and love certainly contributed both to her sympathetic poetic portraits of fallen women and to her decision to join the work of

2. H. Goodwyn, *A Midnight Visit to the Haunts of the Homeless* (London: John Elliott, 1859), 12.

3. See, for example, "The Vices of the Street," *Meliora* 1 (1858–59): 70–79; and "The Social Evil," *Meliora* 3 (1860–61): 145–57.

4. A. O. Charles, *The Female Mission to the Fallen* (London: John Henry and James Parker, 1860), 13.

reclaiming the real women of her society. In a sense, by leaving the literary characters alive and by helping at Highgate penitentiary, Rossetti refrains from condemning these women; thus, in a sense she refuses to cast the first stone.

Before continuing this discussion of the fallen women of Rossetti's poetry, it is important to consider the actual fallen women of Highgate penitentiary and the work Rossetti did at this institution. Such information suggests that while Rossetti certainly viewed these women sympathetically, she did nevertheless see them as sinners who first needed to repent in order to be forgiven. Only by accepting Christ's love could their story be changed.

A letter to Rossetti's friend Amelia Barnard Heimann indicates that by August 1859, Rossetti had begun her work at the London Diocesan Penitentiary of St. Mary Magdalene's on Highgate Hill.[5] This institution was established as the deed reads, "for the reception and reformation of penitent fallen women with a view to their ultimate establishment in some respectable calling."[6] (One should notice here the word "penitent." These women were expected to feel sorry for their sins.) At some point in 1859, Reverend Burrows preached a sermon at Christ Church on behalf of the London Diocesan Penitentiary, and a collection was taken. Perhaps this sermon was instrumental in Rossetti's decision to involve herself in the work of saving her fallen sisters. Clearly, she would have seen such work as sanctioned by her parish church and her family, for the records indicate that her aunt, Eliza Polidori, and William Michael Rossetti contributed to the institution in 1860.

At this institution Rossetti most likely met women from various classes and in various stages of fall from society, for the warden John Oliver con-

5. Christina Rossetti to Amelia Barnard Heimann, August 3, 1859, *The Collected Letters of Christina Rossetti,* ed. Antony H. Harrison, 4 vols. (Charlottesville: University Press of Virginia, 1997), 1:124–25.

6. Deed for Establishing the London Diocesan Penitentiary, Guildhall Library, London, MS 18532. My information on St. Mary Magdalene's is based primarily on the annual reports held at Guildhall Library (MS 18535) and on the annual reports of the Church Penitentiary Association, an organization founded in 1852 to encourage the establishment of such homes for fallen women and to assist in their maintenance. The Church Penitentiary Association has evolved into the Church Moral Aid Association. I should like to thank this association for allowing me to consult its records.

sidered "only those cases involving a confirmed habit of intoxication as hopeless."[7] The women of Highgate, however, would most likely not have included any dying of syphilis (there was no infirmary, and women who arrived ill were usually sent elsewhere), nor were unwed mothers admitted. The ninth annual report (1860–1861) of the Church Penitentiary Association indicates that the governing board decided that although unwed mothers did indeed need help, such cases could be provided for through "private sources." Since St. Mary Magdalene's received grants from this organization, it seems likely that this resolution had some bearing on its admission policy.

After a stay of not more than two years, during which time the women received training in needlework, laundry, cleaning, and kitchen work, the penitents left the home and often went into domestic service, the penitentiary having found them what the annual reports refer to as "good situations." In other words, proper middle class families did hire these reformed prostitutes. In fact, the warden's report for 1862 states, "Applications for servants from respectable private families far exceed the means of supply."[8] The annual reports also indicate that some women were "returned to friends," and the report for 1862 even includes mention that one penitent was married "from the House." Obviously, these records contradict the commonly held belief that a fallen woman was doomed to die or that she was forever outcast from society. However, a central component of the rhetoric of this movement to save fallen women was the irreversible fall. Repeatedly, in sermon and tract, readers and listeners are reminded that if they do not contribute to the establishing of "houses of mercy," the term applied to such institutions, their fallen sisters are doomed to both physical and, more tragically, spiritual death.

Although the very practical work of training these women in "industrial occupation" was a central part of the penitentiary system, it is important to remember that a firm belief in the need to help save the fallen woman's soul was behind the movement. As the sixth annual report of St. Mary Magdalene's stresses, the "main profit to be gained" is the "sav-

7. "House of Mercy," *English Woman's Journal* 1 (1858): 24.
8. The warden's report for 1862 can be found in "St. Mary Magdalene, Park House, Highgate," *St. Michael's Parish Magazine* (January 1864): 16–17.

ing of the soul of the poor penitent." Whether she had fallen merely once or had been earning her living on the streets for some time, she was seen as a sinner, and she had to be brought back to her Redeemer. Not surprisingly, therefore, religious instruction was a central part of the daily routine of the institution. As well as recording how many inmates were hired as servants, the records also indicate how many were either baptized or confirmed and how many received Holy Communion for the first time.

As a woman, Rossetti would have seen herself especially called to this work of redeeming her fallen sisters. Some in her society argued that pure women should have nothing to do with the fallen (it is interesting to note that Dante Gabriel Rossetti's "Jenny" implies such a message), whereas the argument presented by those clergymen involved in the establishment of these houses of mercy was just the opposite. One of the major points stressed by Revs. John Armstrong and Thomas Carter, two prominent figures in the early stages of the penitentiary movement, was that the old system of caring for the penitent with a paid matron and a few visiting ladies was not working. A new system was needed in which a special type of self-sacrificing pure woman played the central role: "They [the penitents] need some such sisters to be ever at their side, watching them in weak moments, encouraging them in seasons of over-whelming gloom, checking outbreaks of temper and light words, directing and controlling their conversation, moving about them like a moral atmosphere, acting on them in many ways of indirect as well as of direct influence, being present with them at their meals, their work, their relaxations; not as spies or jailers, but as friends and guardians." Not surprisingly, when the establishment of the London Diocesan Penitentiary was announced in the *Times,* the article emphasized the contribution unfallen women could make: "Such disinterested services are precisely those which would be most valuable in such a case, by causing the penitent to feel that she was not without the sympathy of those from whom she had been long taught to expect only aversion and contempt."[9] With such views being supported by members of the Anglican Church, it is not surprising that some of the early orders of Anglican sisterhoods,

9. John Armstrong, "The Church and Her Female Penitents," *Christian Remembrancer* 17 (January 1849): 9; *London Times,* January 25, 1854, 8.

such as the Society of St. John the Baptist, considered its special work
that of saving fallen women.

Although the community of women running St. Mary Magdalene's
did not evolve into a fully established religious order, the women in
charge did form a kind of organized sisterhood. Each "sister" went
through a probationary period before being "fully admitted," at which
time a special religious service was held, and although "every sister was
free to leave her office," she had to "promise to be bound by and observe
all the rules and regulations of the Institution." The institution itself had
much the atmosphere of a convent. Each sister wore a black dress with a
cap of "soft pure muslin" and a "string of black beads and a cross" about
her neck; rules of silence were often enforced; religious services were
held several times a day; and the building itself was behind high walls and
thus set apart from the rest of the Highgate community.[10] Considering
how sympathetic Rossetti was to the revival of Anglican sisterhoods, it is
not at all surprising that she associated herself with the women, both pure
and fallen, of Highgate penitentiary.

By 1860 Rossetti was what was actually referred to as an "associate sister." St. Mary Magadelene's first annual report provides some insight into
what this title meant: "Some ladies are engaged as 'Associate Sisters,' in
promoting the interests of the institution in the several spheres of life and
society to which they belong." From a letter to Pauline Trevelyan, it is
known that Rossetti did get involved in encouraging people to attend a
sort of open house at which money was raised, and her letters also suggest
she stayed at Highgate for several days at a time, taking part in the work.
Thus far, no biographer has yet identified precisely what Rossetti did.
However, since the inmates were not allowed to talk to the sisters of their
past lives, we can assume that Rossetti was not the recipient of confessions or of any sort of personal tales of distress. A reasonable assumption
is that Rossetti, who had been involved in her parish Sunday school, took
part in the religious instruction of the inmates. St. Mary Magdalene's also
offered instruction in reading, writing, and arithmetic, and thus she well
may have been engaged in these lessons as well. Finally, since reading to
the inmates while they worked was often part of the daily routine in a
house of mercy, we might assume that Rossetti was at times called upon

10. Guildhall Library, MS 18532; "House of Mercy," 15.

as a reader. The existing records of St. Mary Magdalene's indicate that a library was available for the use of the inmates and the sisters. Unfortunately, no mention is made of specific texts. However, research done on the Magdalene Hospital, one of the early institutions founded for reclaiming prostitutes, provides some clues. First, any literature provided for the inmates and the matrons had to be approved by the warden, and second, the available reading material was primarily, as one might expect, of an explicitly religious nature, such as sermons and texts of religious instruction; however, some poetry was also allowed.[11]

D. M. R. Bentley has conjectured that Rossetti wrote "Goblin Market" with the fallen women of Highgate in mind; that is, he suggests that we see Laura as one of the fallen inmates and Lizzie as the self-sacrificing sister intent on saving her. Bentley also conjectures that Rossetti may have actually read this poem to the inmates. Early reviews of "Goblin Market" indicate that Victorians saw in this poem of forbidden fruit a tale of temptation and redemption. One reviewer even suggested that the poem might be read as "an allegory against the pleasure of sinful love."[12] If texts read to the inmates of Highgate had to be approved, one might reasonably imagine that the warden, John Oliver, found such a tale acceptable, although it is hard to imagine the shy Rossetti reading her work to others in any sort of public forum. However, the movement to save fallen women was clearly one of the sources of this complex poem, for although there is no concrete evidence as yet that Rossetti had actually started her work at Highgate by April 1859, which is the date of composition of "Goblin Market," certainly by the spring of 1859, Rossetti was well aware that her church was calling for pure women to help their fallen sisters.

One might reasonably wonder if the time Rossetti spent at Highgate

11. Christina Rossetti to William Michael Rossetti, London, October 25, 1861, *The Collected Letters of Christina Rossetti,* ed. Harrison, 1:26; Herbert Fuller Compston, *The Magdalene Hospital: The Story of a Great Charity* (London: Society for Promoting Christian Knowledge, 1917), 183–84.

12. D. M. R. Bentley, "The Meretricious and the Meritorious in *Goblin Market*: A Conjecture and an Analysis," in *The Achievement of Christina Rossetti,* ed. David A. Kent (Ithaca: Cornell University Press, 1987), 57–81; Mrs. Charles Eliot Norton, "'The Angel in the House' and 'The [sic] Goblin Market,'" *Macmillan's Magazine* 8 (September 1863): 401.

penitentiary with these fallen women in any way altered her own poetry. On first consideration it would appear not, for "Cousin Kate," "Margery," and "'The Iniquity,'" composed after she began her direct involvement in the cause of saving her fallen sisters, are all similar to "Light Love" and "An Apple-Gathering," what we might consider the pre-Highgate poems. As mentioned earlier, all five of these poems blur the distinctions between pure and fallen. One also finds in these post-Highgate poems the same condemnation of the fallen man and the same sympathy evoked for the fallen woman. However, both the monologue "'The Iniquity,'" written five to six years after Rossetti began her work at Highgate, and "The Sinner's Own Fault? So It Was," a much revised version of "Margery" published approximately twenty years later, more directly challenge Victorian readers' tendency to set themselves apart from the fallen woman's story. In other words, both these poems turn a reader's eyes from the individual sinner to society, and even to the reader's own self as a member of that society. Of course, we cannot conclude that Highgate was the only cause of such development in Rossetti's thought, but we can conclude that the time at Highgate did not alter her initial sympathy for these women, nor did it alter her reluctance to judge them. Quite possibly, being among those her society so harshly condemned encouraged in her a stronger sense of communal guilt and the need for all, as Rossetti urges in "The Sinner's Own Fault," to "mend and pray" (*CP*, 2:308).

In "'The Iniquity of the Fathers,'" Rossetti raises questions of responsibility: Is a child to be punished for the sins of the parents? Would God, a loving and merciful father, inflict such punishment on an innocent child? Is the concept of illegitimacy itself man-made? Rossetti wrote this long narrative poem during a time of increasing public concern over the number of illegitimate children being born and what was happening to them.[13] (Rossetti's own experience at Highgate, an institution that did not accept unwed mothers, would have made her quite aware that few institutions existed at that time that would help an unwed mother and child.) Rossetti had drawn attention to the subject by including an illegit-

---

13. For a discussion of the Victorian response to infanticide, see Ann R. Higginbotham, "'Sin of the Age': Infanticide and Illegitimacy in Victorian London," *Victorian Studies* 32 (spring 1989): 319–37.

imate baby in "Light Love" and "Cousin Kate"; however, in those two poems it is possible to see the child as merely the conventional literary device to prove the woman's shame. In "'The Iniquity,'" such a reading is more difficult, for the illegitimate child has grown up and can speak of her own impressions of her mother's fall and father's sin.

As the title suggests, Rossetti draws more attention to the guilt of the father than the mother. In the daughter's eyes her father, a man she has apparently never met, is far more guilty than her mother. Margaret, the illegitimate daughter, accuses the father of having "wrought [her] Mother's shame" and of setting a "snare" to catch her mother's youth. The daughter's impression of her mother, however, is quite different. First, Margaret stresses her mother's goodness: "Poor people say she's good / . . . and she's the comforter / of many sick and sad" (*CP,* 1:166). A reader might conclude that the mother's charitable work among the poor is her self-imposed penance for her sin, and thus she appears as a repentant fallen woman. The only fault of which she is now guilty is that of not being able to tell her daughter the truth, that is, admit to her that she, the lady of the manor, is her mother. The mother seems unable to face the public humiliation of such an admission. Yet the daughter, while troubled by that silence, understands it. Margaret stresses what would happen if the mother's secret were known: she would be set "in the dust, / Lorn with no comforter" (1:174). The daughter appears to see such punishment as too severe. Furthermore, she sees the society that would inflict it as hypocritical:

> The decent world would thrust
> Its finger out at her,
> Not much displeased I think
> To make a nine days' stir.

(1:175)

The implication is that the "decent world" is not so decent in the pleasure it would take in gossiping about the lady of the manor. Moreover, while the "decent world" would exile the mother forever, Margaret does not imagine that God would. In the daughter's mind, the lie her mother lives will not keep her out of paradise. Margaret seems to hope that after death her mother will finally recognize her, that is, claim her as her daughter: "Mother, in Paradise, / You'll see with clearer eyes" (1:175). Her father, as one might expect, is not part of her fantasies of heaven, and although the daughter does not imagine him in hell, she does "almost curse" him.

The daughter quite clearly places more blame on her father than on her mother for the fact that she has not had the earthly family love she desires, especially from her mother. Primarily because of her father's sin, Margaret rejects the family structure as offering her an identity. In other words, she rejects marriage. Even though her mother clearly wants her to marry, presumably so she might have the happy life she herself did not have, and even though Margaret has definite marriage possibilities, she vows she will remain single:

> I'll not be wooed for pelf:
> I'll not blot out my shame
> With any man's good name;
> But nameless as I stand,
> My hand is my own hand,
> And nameless as I came
> I go to the dark land.
>
> (1:178)

Her father did not give her his name, and thus she will not take any man's name. She then turns, as the female speakers of "The Lowest Room" and "Light Love" do, to look after death for a righting of earthly injustices. Again, the end of the woman's story will only be read on the Last Day:

> "All equal in the grave"—
> I bide my time till then:
> "All equal before God"—
> Today I feel His rod,
> Tomorrow He may save:
>                    Amen.
>
> (1:178)

While some of Rossetti's readers might have found denying the illegitimate daughter a happy marriage ending an appropriate sign of disapproval of the mother's fall, Rossetti attempts to undercut that response with her focus on equality. If all are equal in the grave and, more important, also before God, why does society have the right to make such distinctions between legitimate and illegitimate children and, similarly, between pure women and penitent fallen women? Rossetti underscores the validity of this message of equality by indicating that "all equal before God" is not a text the illegitimate child writes herself but rather one she recalls the rector speaking, and one Rossetti herself probably used, intending to echo St. Paul's epistle to the Galatians: "There is neither Jew nor Greek, there is neither bond nor free, there is neither male nor female: for ye are all one in Christ Jesus. And if ye be Christ's, then are ye Abraham's seed, and heirs according to the promise" (Gal. 3:28–29). In other words, all are legitimate children of God. Furthermore, this recollection of the rector's words leads immediately to the last three lines of the poem, which form a sort of illegitimate child's prayer (notice that the very last word of the poem is "amen"), a prayer reminding readers that God is the ultimate judge ("Today I feel His rod") and redeemer ("Tomorrow He may save"). These last lines focus the poem on Rossetti's "real" world of the spirit, not the "waxwork" world, where even the mother–child relationship, a relationship the Victorians celebrated in countless sentimental ways if the mother was married, could be marred by the harsh codes of a society, one that appeared only to judge and not to save.[14] By the end of the poem, the title well might be seen to refer not just to the sins of the biological father, his seduction and betrayal of a young woman and his apparent refusal to accept any responsibility for his child, but also to the sins of the whole society. The fathers of Victorian society, that is, those who had power, were failing to care for all children.

Rossetti's title is taken from Exod. 20:5, a portion of the Second Commandment, which speaks against idolatry: "Thou shalt not bow down thyself to them [graven images], nor serve them: for I the Lord thy God am a jealous God, visiting the iniquity of the fathers upon the children unto the third and fourth generation of them that hate me." When Rossetti first published this poem she used as the title "Under the Rose,"

14. See *Time Flies* (36) for Rossetti's distinction between this "waxwork" world and the "substantial eternal world."

which recalls the Latin phrase *sub rosa* (in secret); the biblical text "the iniquity of the fathers upon the children" was placed beneath the title as a motto. In her 1875 edition, Rossetti replaced the initial title with the motto, thus giving the biblical text far more prominence. Christian theologians do not accept the concept that children should be punished for their parents' sins, for such a concept is repudiated in Ezek. 18:14–20 and in Christ's message regarding the blind child (see John 9:2). In *The Face of the Deep,* when discussing the commandments, Rossetti herself finds in Ezek. 18:14–17 a "door of hope" for the children of sinners (397). Certainly, her sympathetic depiction of this child born "under the rose" indicates that she did not want to see in Exod. 20:5 justification for punishing the innocent for another's sin. Rossetti's comments in *Letter and Spirit* suggest, however, that she did see sin as having consequences that could reach far beyond the individual sinner: "In the Second [Commandment] each man is still addressed by himself, yet the tone and colour (so to say) of this Commandment is multitudinous: 'the third and fourth generation' are imperilled by transgression" (89). Rossetti's title thus draws her reader's attention to the possibility that a father's action could imperil a child, and the text of the poem itself makes it clear that such endangering of the innocent is a sign of a flawed society, one that embraces a flawed concept of fatherhood. Significantly, in *Letter and Spirit,* Rossetti concludes her thoughts on the "multitudinous" nature of this commandment with a plea for the children: "Hard indeed must be that heart which cannot be moved 'for the children's sake'" (90).

Years after her experience at Highgate ended but during a time when Rossetti was still showing an interest in combating the Great Social Evil, she returned to "Margery," a poem that explores the community's responsibility for the fallen woman who was only a year ago, "a child."[15] The very first line of the poem directly questions the reader: "What shall we do with Margery?" (*CP,* 3:289). In 1885, when Rossetti returned to this poem, one she had never published, she borrowed from it in order to write a poem with the explicit message that not only were all human beings sinners but also that one might well have contributed to another's fall from grace:

15. According to William Michael Rossetti, his sister worked at Highgate until about 1870; however, Rossetti's most recent biographer, Jan Marsh, suggests 1864 as a more likely date.

The sinner's own fault? So it was.
   If every own fault found us out,
   Dogged us and hedged us round about,
   What comfort should we take, because
   Not half our due we thus wrung out?

Clearly his own fault. Yet I think
   My fault in part, who did not pray,
   But lagged, and would not lead the way.
I, haply, proved his missing link.
God help us both to mend and pray.

(CP, 2:308)

The first stanza of this untitled poem is stanza seven of "Margery," with a significant pronoun change: "her own fault" has become "his own fault." By making this slight revision, Rossetti removes the issue of gender from the fallen woman's story in that she becomes simply a sinner and removes the focus on any specific sin, sexual or otherwise. Moreover, in the second stanza, Rossetti begins to blur the distinction between this sinner and herself by considering the possibility that she played a role in the sinner's fall. (I am here reading the speaker as Rossetti herself, for the personal nature of *Time Flies,* a devotional diary, suggests such a reading.) Thus, Rossetti shifts the emphasis from judgment of the other to judgment of the self. And as another entry in *Time Flies* indicates, for Rossetti the lines between sinner and self, and by implication between sinner and reader, might well be nonexistent:

> All sinners, all shortcomers, all criminals, all are to be beloved, if not as friends then as enemies.
> But which of us is the lover and which the beloved in this connexion? The best of us is a sinner, the worst of us may become a saint.
> If we love all, we shall be the less likely to class erroneously either ourself or our neighbour. (69)

This message of loving the sinner and simultaneously recognizing one's own guilt is repeated throughout *Time Flies.*[16] Moreover, "The sin-

16. For example, see also Rossetti's entries in *Time Flies* for April 14 and December 4.

ner's own fault? so it was" appears in *Time Flies* as the devotional reading for July 21, the day before Mary Magdalene's feast day and thus serves as an introduction to the comments Rossetti then makes, in the July 22nd entry, on this sinner, who through love and forgiveness became a saint. Before concluding this discussion of the fallen woman, I will give some attention to Rossetti's response to Mary Magdalene, for the movement to save fallen women often made reference to this saint. For example, the cover of each annual report of St. Mary Magdalene's at Highgate displayed a sketch of Mary Magdalene with her box of ointment kneeling beneath an image of a forgiving Christ.

Although Rossetti quite possibly was not opposed to associating Mary Magdalene with the crusade to save fallen women, significantly, when Rossetti actually mentions this saint by name she refrains from any reference, even a veiled one, to sexual sin. In an early poem, "Divine and Human Pleading," she simply refers to Magdalene's "great transgression / The sin of the other time" (*CP*, 3:90). Rossetti seems to have been quite aware that the biblical record did not name Magdalene's sin, and to a certain extent she takes advantage of that fact to suit her purposes. (The image of Magdalene as the penitent whore is derived from the earlier Christian commentators; nowhere in the Bible is Mary Magdalene's sin actually named.)[17] Since the biblical record does not require that Rossetti speak of Magdalene's sexuality, she does not. For Rossetti, Mary Magdalene was to be associated not with sin but with forgiveness, and not with the body but with the soul.

In her comments on the saint's life in *Time Flies,* she stresses love rather than sin:

> A record of this Saint is a record of love. She ministered to the Lord of her substance, she stood by the Cross, she sat over against the Sepulchre, she sought Christ in the empty grave, and found Him and was found of Him in the contiguous garden.
>
> Yet this is that same Mary Magdalene out of whom aforetime He had cast seven devils.

17. For a detailed analysis of the image of Mary Magdalene as she has appeared in church history, art, and literature, see Susan Haskins, *Mary Magdalene: Myth and Metaphor* (New York: Harcourt Brace, 1993).

Nevertheless, the golden cord of love we are contemplating did all along continue unbroken in its chief strand: for before she loved Him, He loved her. (139–40)

The details of Magdalene's past sins are of little interest to Rossetti; it is her relationship with Christ that engages the poet's attention. Not surprisingly, therefore, she seems to have been particularly drawn to the biblical texts in which Mary Magdalene is said to be the first to have seen the risen Christ. In *Seek and Find,* when commenting on "a few memorable nights and days in the careers of New Testaments Saints," Rossetti writes at length about this moment:

> On the first day of the week while it was yet dark St. Mary Magdalene sought the sepulchre, and outlingered all other lovers of Jesus save angels only; with whom she held high converse, being as it were the very bride of the Song of Songs (v. 9,10): "What is thy Beloved more than another beloved, O thou fairest among women? . . . . [ellipsis Rossetti's] My Beloved is white and ruddy, the chiefest among ten thousand." And none but she out of whom went seven devils was the first to behold our risen Saviour (St. John xx. 1–18; St. Mark xvi.9). (231–32)

In *The Face of the Deep,* Rossetti again refers to this meeting outside the sepulchre between Christ and Magdalene, and this time she encourages the reader to see in Magdalene's meeting with the risen Christ a glimpse of the "beatified life" to come when each "saved soul," being fully recognized, fully identified by Christ, will achieve a full and satisfying acceptance of self: "When Christ shall call each happy, heavenly soul by name, as once He called 'Mary' in an earthly garden, then each will perceive herself to be that which He calls her; and will no more question her own designation than did those primitive creatures whom the first Adam named in the inferior Paradise" (*FD,* 73). Rossetti's reading of Mary Magdalene as representative of each saved soul and, similarly, her comparison of the Magdalene with the bride of the Song of Songs are not original. (For example, Hippolytus' third-century commentary on the Song of Songs offers a similar interpretation.) However, such associations are startling when considered in the context of the Victorian tendency to associate Magdalene with the prostitutes of the London streets. Thus, while others were using the image of Magdalene as an image of female sexuality and sin, Rossetti not only refrains from contributing to the continuation of such images but also directs her society away from its preoccupation with woman's sin, especially sexual sin, toward a consideration of a woman's potential redemption.

Consistently, from Rossetti's fallen woman ballads of the 1850s and 1860s to her later devotional prose and poetry, Rossetti directs the reader's attention away from seeing the sinner as other, as separate and apart from the rest of the human community. Although her faith certainly led her to see the fallen women of her time as sinners, for Rossetti that was not the end of their story. Not only could each fallen woman become a saint, but each individual should also aspire to be like the penitent and loving Mary Magdalene.

In Rossetti's treatment of Eve, the first fallen woman, one finds a similar emphasis on divine forgiveness, an emphasis that again turns the reader from seeing the sinful woman as other and apart to seeing her as very much a part of the human community.

*five*

# ROSSETTI'S EVE AND THE
# WOMAN QUESTION

✝

ROSSETTI'S RESPONSE TO THE WOMAN QUESTION WAS COMPLEX
and, as it might appear to modern readers, contradictory. Her support of
Anglican sisterhoods, her questioning of marriage as woman's highest
goal, and even her compassionate response to prostitutes all indicate that
she repeatedly questioned those domestic and sexual ideologies that
helped to keep Victorian women in a second-class position. And although there is at present no evidence that she ever campaigned or
signed any petition for the expansion of women's rights, her early association with the women of Langham Place Circle indicates that she well
might have been in favor of increasing educational and work opportunities for women, two of the goals central to this circle's mission.[1] Certainly, her position as a publishing poet, one who very much wanted her
books to sell, suggests that she was willing to accept some mingling of the
public (masculine) and private (feminine) spheres. Yet, ultimately Rossetti must have concluded that some form of limitation on all of Eve's
daughters was just. In 1889, she signed a petition against granting women
parliamentary suffrage, and in both prose and poetry, she reminds women

---

1. For a discussion of Rossetti's connection with the Langham Place Circle, see my
article "Christina Rossetti and *The English Woman's Journal,*" *Journal of Pre-Raphaelite Studies,* n.s., 3 (spring 1994): 20–24.

of what was to her a fact, that Eve was created as a helpmeet for Adam. To understand these seeming inconsistencies and apparent contradictions, we need to examine in detail Rossetti's view of Eve, for behind all her views on woman's rights, duties, and privileges in this world stands the image of the first mother.

In *The Face of the Deep*, during a discussion of "feminine character," Rossetti places before the reader the Virgin Mary, Eve, and Mary Magdalene, as if in a triptych:

> Eve exhibits one extreme of feminine character, the Blessed Virgin the opposite extreme. Eve parleyed with a devil: holy Mary "was troubled" at the salutation of an Angel. Eve sought knowledge: Mary instruction. Eve aimed at self-indulgence: Mary at self-oblation. Eve, by disbelief and disobedience, brought sin to the birth: Mary, by faith and submission, Righteousness.
>
> And yet, even as at the foot of the Cross, St. Mary Magdalene, out of whom went seven devils, stood beside the "lily among thorns," the Mother of sorrows: so (I humbly hope and trust) amongst all saints of all time will stand before the Throne, Eve the beloved first Mother of us all. Who that has loved and revered her own immediate dear mother, will not echo the hope? (310)

Rossetti begins by echoing the patristic writings that contrast Eve's temptation with Mary's annunciation, a contrast often made by the church fathers to show how Eve's sin was ransomed through Mary.[2] Rossetti at first appears to be using this traditional antithesis so as to set Mary before her female readers as the woman to follow and Eve as the woman to shun. Certainly, Mary's obedience, selflessness, and unquestioning faith are all being pointed to as ideal feminine qualities. By the end of the second paragraph, however, one realizes that Eve has actually been positioned as the central figure in this triptych, and not as the cautionary image one might expect given the comparison with Mary, but rather as the redeemed woman. Similarly, Rossetti concludes her point on "feminine character" not by telling women to emulate the mother of Christ,

---

2. For a concise discussion of Mary as the New Eve, see Hilda Graef, *The Devotion to Our Lady* (New York: Hawthorne Books, 1963), 17–21.

but by encouraging her readers to hope that the "beloved first Mother" will be among the saints on the Last Day.

Typically, Eve is portrayed as at best the foolish, weak woman who caused the fall of all humankind or, at worst, the evil temptress who seduced Adam into sin.[3] Rossetti's depiction of Eve as the beloved mother standing before God's throne is in striking opposition to such misogynistic representations of womanhood. Indeed, Rossetti's association of the first fallen woman with motherhood appears especially striking when one considers the Victorian period's celebration of wedded motherhood as the highest form of feminine purity.[4] Repeatedly, in both prose and poetry, Rossetti depicts Eve sympathetically, and her focus on Eve as mother is at the center of this portrayal. Although as we shall see, Rossetti accepted the reading of Genesis that saw Eve as created from Adam's side in order to be his helpmeet, she was more drawn to conceptualizing Eve as the mother of all humanity than as the wife of Adam.

When exploring Rossetti's depiction of Eve, it is important to remember that for Rossetti, Eve was an actual historical personage. She was indeed the first mother, and therefore, as Rossetti reminds the reader in "Listening," she is "your ancestress and mine" (*CP*, 3:236). In *The Face of the Deep*, Rossetti indirectly points out that because Eve was the mother of all, she was therefore also the mother of Jesus Christ: "His [Christ's] Crown is a Crown of thorns transcending any which Solomon in all his glory put on. His mother crowned Him therewith, Eve the mother of us all, Eve whose wilfulness brought in death" (65). Significantly, Rossetti's longest poetic treatment of the Fall, simply entitled "Eve," does not focus on Eve and Lucifer or even Eve and Adam but rather on Eve and Abel. In other words, in this poem the loss of Eden is set before the reader not in any of its typical images, such as Lucifer tempting Eve or Eve tempting Adam or Adam and Eve in exile with the flaming sword barring their return to Eden. Rather, Rossetti depicts Eve as the sorrowful mother, grieving over the body of her son Abel:

3. For a more detailed discussion of Eve as depicted in Western culture, see J. A. Phillips, *Eve: The History of an Idea* (San Francisco: Harper and Row, 1984).
4. See Lynda Nead, *Myths of Sexuality: Representations of Women in Victorian Britain* (Oxford: Basil Blackwell, 1988), 26.

Thus she sat weeping,
Thus Eve our mother,
Where one lay sleeping
Slain by his brother.

(*CP*, 1:157)

Eve's anguish is underscored by the responsibility she bears and, moreover, accepts:

I, Eve, sad mother
Of all who must live,
I, not another,
Plucked bitterest fruit to give
My friend, husband, lover; —
O wanton eyes, run over;
Who but I should grieve?—
Cain hath slain his brother:
Of all who must die mother,
Miserable Eve!

(1:157)

She admits that it was she who let death into the world: "I chose the tree of death." Significantly, she does not blame Cain at all. Unlike Byron's Eve in his verse drama *Cain*, a possible precursor text, Rossetti's Eve, in a sense, curses only herself:

Hadst thou but said me nay,
Adam, my brother,
I might have pined away;
I, but none other:
God might have let thee stay
Safe in our garden,
By putting me away
Beyond all pardon.

(1:157)

Because she condemns only herself, she remains throughout the poem a sympathetic figure ennobled by her grief.

CHRISTINA ROSSETTI

In this regard, Rossetti's Eve resembles the representation of Eve to be found in two other precursor texts: Elizabeth Barrett Browning's "A Drama of Exile" and Solomon Gessner's *The Death of Abel*. Gessner's prose narrative was first published in German in 1762; however, an English translation was available in 1833, and quite possibly Rossetti was familiar with it. She most certainly was familiar with Browning's "A Drama of Exile." Although Browning does not include the story of Cain and Abel in her verse drama, Rossetti's sympathetic portrayal of Eve very much recalls Browning's poem, in that Browning's Eve, like Rossetti's sorrowful mother, is a woman ennobled by grief.[5] However, unlike either of these writers, Rossetti keeps Adam silent. In "Drama of Exile," when Eve berates herself for being the first to sin, Adam calms and comforts her. Similarly, in Gessner's work, Adam also comforts and shares in Eve's sense of guilt. While certainly it is relevant that Rossetti's "Eve" is a less ambitious work than either "A Drama of Exile" or *The Death of Abel* ("Eve" focuses on only a moment in the drama of the Fall, whereas each of the other works has much more scope), the silence of Adam should not be overlooked. Rossetti's Eve addresses him, and so one might imagine Adam as part of the scene, but by keeping him silent, Rossetti keeps the reader focused on Eve as the grieving mother who curses only herself and thus keeps the reader focused on Eve as the noble figure.

Those who share in Eve's grief in Rossetti's poem are the animals: the mouse, cattle, the eagle, larks, bees, the raven, the conies all pause in their daily habits, each in its way "sympathetical" and "answering grief by grief." Having nature mourn with Eve reinforces the association of Eve not with death but life: her sin brought death into the world, but she still is, as her name signifies, the mother of all the living. The only creature who does not mourn, not surprisingly, is the snake, who appears in the concluding lines:

Only the serpent in the dust
Wriggling and crawling,

5. For a reading of Rossetti's "Eve" as a response to Browning, see Antony Harrison, "In the Shadow of E.B.B.: Christina Rossetti and Ideological Estrangement," in Harrison, *Victorian Poets and Romantic Poems* (Charlottesville: University Press of Virginia, 1990), 108–43.

Grinned an evil grin and thrust
His tongue out with its fork.

(*CP*, 1:158)

This final image is especially notable for two reasons. First, it draws
the reader's attention away from Eve as the cause of evil and focuses it
on Lucifer. In Rossetti's version of the Fall, the villain is clearly the devil,
not the grieving mother. Although Abel's murder is a consequence of
Eve's sin, the murder began, so to speak, not with Eve's eating of the
forbidden fruit, but with the devil's temptation of Eve; it began with his
evil "tongue," his evil words. Second, although one might argue that
Rossetti in fact diminishes Satan's role by allotting him only four lines of
description and no words, this diminution should be seen within the
context of Rossetti's views on the depiction of evil, which she makes
quite clear when commenting on Rev. 12:7–9, in verses telling of the
"war in heaven" and the devil's defeat: "Whilst studying the devil I must
take heed that my study become not devilish by reason of sympathy. As
to gaze down a precipice seems to fascinate the gazer towards a shattering
fall; so it is spiritually perilous to gaze on excessive wickedness, lest its
immeasurable scale should fascinate us as if it were colossal without being
monstrous" (*FD*, 321). Not surprisingly, she found Milton's "archangel
ruined" a dangerous representation of evil, one that might seduce the
soul (264, 322).

In contrast to Milton's Lucifer, Rossetti's "serpent in the dust" keeps
evil confined to a small space. If one were to illustrate this poem, the
snake might well appear beneath the major figures so as to occupy only
a small portion of the canvas.[6] Thus, while Rossetti effectively conveys
the sense that the "old serpent," spoken of in Revelation, is the source
of evil, and not the grieving mother, Rossetti does not risk evoking the
reader's sympathy for or interest in Lucifer by allowing him to occupy
our attention for too long. Moreover, the brief phrase "in the dust," recalling as it does Gen. 3:14–15, actually serves not only to keep evil
where it belongs, so to speak, but also points to Satan's ultimate defeat
and to Eve's redemption: From Eve's "seed" would come the Re-

---

6. See, for example, Florence Harrison's illustration of the poem in *Poems by Christina
Rossetti* (London: Blackie and Son, 1910).

deemer, the one who would crush the serpent's head and open the gates of heaven for Adam and Eve and all their children.

Indeed, because the death of Abel is often read as a prototype of Christ's death, the whole poem, not just the last image, points to the hope offered both Eve and all humankind. If one imagines Eve as actually mourning over her son's body, then the scene may also bring to mind that of the pietà. Such an association not only reinforces the depiction of Eve as grieving mother but also further undercuts the typical image of Eve as the evil temptress by associating her with the Virgin Mary. Rossetti clearly preferred to imagine Eve in terms of forgiveness and redemption rather than in terms of sin and the loss of Eden. For example, in "An Afterthought," she describes Eve as "forgiven" and waiting in paradise for the resurrection, and in "That Eden of earth's sunrise cannot vie," the speaker imagines Eve entering heaven transformed into the virtuous woman of the book of Proverbs: "your children rise / And call you blessed, in their glad surmise / Of Paradise" (*CP,* 2:220).

Although Rossetti accepted as fact that Eve's "wilfulness" brought death into the world, she nevertheless appears to have wanted to free the first mother from being associated with death. For example, in two unpublished fragments on Eve, probably written when Rossetti was working on *Seek and Find,* she reveals how strong her desire was to see Eve in terms of life, not death. In commenting on Exod. 1:22 ("And Pharaoh charged all his people, saying, Every son that is born ye shall cast into the river, and every daughter ye shall save alive"), Rossetti writes:

> There seems to be a sense in which from the Fall downwards the penalty of death has been laid on man and of life on woman. To Eve: "I will greatly multiply thy sorrow and thy conception; in sorrow thou shalt bring forth children:"—to Adam: "Unto dust shalt thou return." The mere name *Eve* was "the mother of all living," or it may be (?) of the Living One. May it so be that in this distinction is hidden the true key which supersedes any need of an "Immaculate Conception," that from the father alone is derived the stock and essence of the child; the mother, transmitting her own humanity, contributing no more than the nourishment, development, style so to say. The father active, the mother receptive. Thus dead Adam must be the father of a dead child: the Living God the

Father of the Living Son. Thus "Who can bring a clean thing out of the unclean? Not one,"—would darkly set forth the same immutable fact: (All this I write down craving pity and pardon of God for Xt's sake if I err).[7]

As a devout Anglican, Rossetti did not accept the Roman Catholic doctrine of the Immaculate Conception, that is, that Mary was conceived free of original sin. These comments reflect Rossetti's attempt to explain Christ's sinless nature, by arguing that Adam alone was the transmitter of sin, and therefore since Jesus did not have a mortal father, only a mortal mother, he was born free from sin. In another unpublished note, one in which she turns to St. Paul's comments on Adam, Rossetti again seeks to find in the fact of Christ's sinless nature proof that even though Eve sinned, she was not the transmitter of sin: "That Eve sinned and earned her own death is clear, but we are not told that she brought death upon the human family. 'In Adam all die' writes St. Paul, taking no notice of the guilty woman: again: (Rom. 5.12 ) 'by one man sin entered into the world, and death by sin.'"[8] By interpreting St. Paul's use of the name "Adam" not as a reference to all humanity but as reference to men, Rossetti finds a reading that suits her desire to see Eve as a beloved mother and to free motherhood itself from any association with sin.

Rossetti's published comments on Eve are not as radical as these, but they are just as partial in regard to the first mother. Repeatedly, she stresses that Eve was deceived by Satan and that her very innocence, her lack of guile, made her vulnerable. But Satan was master of "guile," and she was "cajoled" (*TF*, 237). When Satan offered her the fruit, she was innocent, and when she offered the forbidden fruit to Adam, her motives were innocent still. The most striking example of this sympathetic view of Eve's intentions appears in *Letter and Spirit,* as part of Rossetti's com-

7. The original of these notes has apparently been lost; however, they are quoted from in Lona Mosk Packer, *Christina Rossetti* (Berkeley: University of California Press, 1963), 330.

8. Christina Rossetti, "Eve," MS, Troxell Collection, Princeton University Library, Princeton. For an insightful discussion on the significance of this unpublished fragment, see Virginia Sickbert, "'Beloved Mother of Us All': Christina Rossetti's Eve," *Christianity and Literature* 44 (April 1995): 289–312.

mentary on the first commandment. Although lengthy, the passage is important enough to quote in full:

> Eve made a mistake, "being *deceived*" she was in transgression: Adam made no mistake: his was an error of will, hers partly of judgment; nevertheless both proved fatal. Eve, equally with Adam, was created sinless: each had a specially vulnerable point, but this apparently not the same point. It is in no degree at variance with the Sacred Record to picture to ourselves Eve, that first and typical woman, as indulging quite innocently sundry refined tastes and aspirations, a castle-building spirit (if so it may be called), a feminine boldness and directness of aim combined with a no less feminine guessiness as to means. Her very virtues may have opened the door to temptation. By birthright gracious and accessible, she lends an ear to all petitions from all petitioners. She desires to instruct ignorance, to rectify misapprehension: "unto the pure all things are pure," and she never suspects even the serpent. Possibly a trace of blameless infirmity transpires in the wording of her answer, "*lest* ye die," for God had said to the man ". . . in the day that thou eatest thereof thou *shalt surely* die": but such tenderness of spirit seems even lovely in the great first mother of mankind; or it may be that Adam had modified the form, if it devolved on him to declare the tremendous fact to his second self. Adam and Eve reached their goal, the Fall, by different routes. With Eve the serpent discussed a question of conduct, and talked her over to his own side: with Adam, so far as appears, he might have argued the point for ever and gained no vantage; but already he had secured an ally weightier than a score of arguments. Eve may not have argued at all: she offered Adam a share of her own good fortune, and having hold of her husband's heart, turned it in her hand as the rivers of water. Eve preferred various prospects to God's Will: Adam seems to have preferred one person to God: Eve diverted her "mind" and Adam his "heart" from God Almighty. Both courses led to one common result, that is, to one common ruin (Gen. iii). (17–18)

Significantly, in keeping with Rossetti's image of Eve as mother, not temptress, Rossetti does not present the first human sin in sexual terms.

In this passage, for example, she ignores the tradition that had transformed Eve's sin of disobedience to God into one of lust and infidelity to Adam. Similarly, in her comment regarding Adam's "heart," while echoing those church fathers who argued that Adam's sin was to prefer Eve to God, there is nothing in Rossetti's language to invite readers to see Eve as having gained through eating the forbidden fruit a sexual knowledge that allows her to entice Adam into sin. Similarly, in her poetry, when Rossetti speaks of Adam, it is not as Eve's victim but as her loving husband. He was her "treasure" that she took with her when exiled from Eden: "Yet the accustomed hand for leading, / Yet the accustomed heart for love" ("An Afterthought," *CP*, 3:243). Indeed, when Adam appears as a noble figure in Rossetti's verse, it is as a loving husband. For example, in Sonnet 15 of *Later Life*, Rossetti suggests the comforting possibility that Adam's love for Eve was constant:

> Did Adam love his Eve from first to last?
>    I think so; as we love who works us ill,
>    And wounds us to the quick, yet loves us still.
> Love pardons the unpardonable past.

*(CP, 2:144–45)*

Although this image of Eve as wife, "gracious and accessible," still loving and still worthy of love, is in opposition to the more conventional images of the first woman, Rossetti did not go so far as those of her century who saw in Eve a Promethean figure liberating humankind from oppression.[9] The lesson Rossetti found in Genesis for the daughters of Eve was clearly one of obedience, not rebellion. Significantly, Sonnet 15 of *Later Life* begins by echoing St. Paul's interpretation of Eve's role in the Fall (see 1 Tim. 2:12): "Let woman fear to teach and bear to learn, / Remembering the first woman's first mistake" (*CP*, 2:144). Rossetti distanced herself from those who judged Eve's sin as worse than Adam's by concluding that in a sense, it was not a human being's place to "attempt to settle which (if either) committed the greater sin" (*LS*, 56), but she did

---

9. See Barbara Taylor, *Eve and the New Jerusalem: Socialism and Feminism in the Nineteenth Century* (London: Virago Press, 1983), 146–57.

follow those who found in the story of the Fall support for assigning men and women to distinctly separate spheres of work and duty. There are no explicit remarks in Rossetti's devotional prose that speak against educating women. Clearly, however, Rossetti felt that women had to be careful in terms of how they pursued knowledge and how they used that knowledge. The snake had deceived Eve; in Rossetti's mind, that deception meant that when Eve offered the fruit to Adam her motives were pure but that her sin involved an error of "judgement" (LS, 17). In commenting on Eve and Lot's wife, Rossetti writes, "Curiosity [is] a feminine weak point inviting temptation, and doubly likely to facilitate a fall when to indulge it woman affects independence" (FD, 520). Not surprisingly, The Face of the Deep, Rossetti's most ambitious work of devotional prose concludes, "If I have been overbold in attempting such a work as this, I beg pardon" (551). Even though Rossetti's views on Eve were in many ways unconventional and at times even subversive, she nevertheless drew a connection between the limits on women in this world and Eve's sin of disobedience.

For today's readers, perhaps Rossetti's most unsettling acceptance of gender difference is her willingness to find in both the Strange Woman of Proverbs and the Whore of Babylon a special meaning for women. When commenting on the woman whose "steps take hold on hell," she writes, "Solomon meanwhile by warning man against woman has virtually warned woman against herself" (FD, 400). And in "the obscene woman" of the book of Revelation, Rossetti saw an illustration of "the particular foulness, degradation, loathsomeness, to which a perverse rebellious woman because feminine not masculine is liable" (400). However, although Rossetti accepted the association of woman with temptation, it is important to notice that these harlot figures, as with Eve, were not seen by Rossetti as representative of lust. Rather, she read them as emblems of female disobedience, of diverting the mind from God. Finally, in regard to both these feminine figures, she concludes, "We daughters of Eve may beyond her sons be kept humble by that common voice which makes temptation feminine. Woman is a mighty power for good or for evil. She constrains though she cannot compel. Potential for evil, it becomes her to beware and forbear; potential for good, to spend herself and be spent for her brethren" (357–58). Clearly, because of Eve's "lapse," Rossetti saw the woman's way to salvation as different from that of man: having the power to influence but not to rule, woman must be humble and self-sacrificing, always putting the one loved before self. In other words, women were to earn salvation through love. In her poem "All Thy Works Praise Thee, O Lord," Rossetti gives the following lines to women:

> God makes our service love, and makes our wage
> Love: so we wend on patient pilgrimage,
> Extolling Him by love from age to age.

(CP, 2:137)

Rossetti's interest in Eve, both in her sin and her redemption, may seem quite apart from the major issues of the Victorian period, but it actually places her very much in the middle of numerous public debates about one of the period's central issues—the woman question. During the years in which attempts were made to widen the feminine sphere, there was much discussion of Eve, her creation, and her role in the Fall. If one concluded that Genesis clearly proved that Eve was indeed more at fault than Adam and, moreover, that woman was innately inferior to man, then one could easily justify woman's second-class status on earth. As late as 1884, for example, John William Burgon, an Anglican clergyman, argued that Genesis offered ample proof of "woman's inferiority," and that therefore women should not be allowed the same education as men: a woman's place was in the home and only in the home.[10]

Considering that Rossetti felt a strong desire to see Eve as a beloved mother who would one day be equal to the Virgin Mary, while at the same time accepting the interpretation of Eve as disobedient daughter whose curiosity and wilfulness led to the loss of Eden, we can see why Rossetti's response to the woman question was complex, conflicted, and at times, perhaps, even contradictory. In the late 1870s, when Augusta Webster urged her to support parliamentary suffrage for women, Rossetti's lengthy response reveals the tensions she felt: "Does it not appear as if the Bible was based upon an understood unalterable distinction between men and women, their position, duties, privileges? Not arrogating

---

10. John William Burgon, *To Educate Young Women like Young Men, and with Young Men—A Thing Inexpedient and Immodest* (Oxford: Parker, 1884).

to myself but most earnestly desiring to attain to the character of a humble orthodox Xtian, so it does appear to me; not merely under the Old but also under the New Dispensation." This letter to Webster is often quoted by those who wish to emphasize Rossetti's feminist leanings, for as Rossetti elaborates on her reason for refusing, she reveals that she is able to imagine female ministers of Parliament:

> On the other hand if female rights are sure to be overborne for lack of female voting influence, then I confess I feel disposed to shoot ahead of my instructresses, and to assert that female M.P.'s are only right and reasonable. Also I take exceptions at the exclusion of married women from the suffrage,—for who so apt as Mothers—all previous arguments allowed for the moment—to protect the interests of themselves and of their offsprings? I do think if anything ever does sweep away the barrier of sex, and make the female not a giantess or a heroine but at once and full grown a hero and giant, it is that mighty maternal love which makes little birds and little beasts as well as little women matches for very big adversaries.[11]

Certainly, there are signs in this letter of conflicted thoughts and feelings. Although Rossetti's reading of the Bible tells her that men and women should occupy separate spheres of duties and influence, she does indicate that she believes that women nevertheless still have "rights." Moreover, her thoughts on maternal love indicate that Rossetti could at least entertain in her imagination a time when women might be considered equal to men in this world.

Refusing to lend her support to the cause of suffrage was perhaps not an easy decision, but apparently it is one of which she became more certain in time. In 1889, she was actually willing to take a public stand against suffrage. Sometime during the summer of that year, Rossetti sent her name and address to the journal *Nineteenth Century* as an indication that she agreed with the sentiments expressed in "An Appeal Against Female Suffrage," a document drafted by Mrs. Humphry Ward and first signed by 104 women. At the end of this article appears the following

11. Quoted in Mackenzie Bell, *Christina Rossetti: A Biographical and Critical Study* (Boston: Roberts Brothers, 1898), 124.

invitation and request from the editor: "In furtherance of the foregoing Appeal—which has hitherto been only shown privately to a few persons—the accompanying proposed protest is laid before the readers of *Nineteenth Century*, with the request that such ladies among them as agree with it will be kind enough to sign the opposite page and return it, when detached, to the Editor of this Review." The accompanying proposed protest reads as follows: "The undersigned protest, strongly against the proposed Extension of the Parliamentary Franchise to Women, which they believe would be a measure distasteful to the great majority of women of the country—unnecessary—and mischievous both to themselves and to the State."[12] In the August issue of this magazine, this statement appears again, under the title "A Woman's Protest Against Female Suffrage," and is followed by the names and addresses of approximately two thousand women. Rossetti's name and address at the time, 30 Torrington Square, can be found in this list.

Examining the full statement of the appeal as it first appeared offers some insight into why Rossetti apparently saw female suffrage as "mischievous." Although it describes all the improvements in woman's position thus far as "cordially welcome," this appeal calls for the "emancipation process" to cease, arguing that to allow women into the political arena would tend "to blunt the special moral qualities of women, and so lessen the national reserves of moral force."[13] We might see this argument as a strategy to keep women out of politics, but it is important not to overlook the power it does assign them: They were to help civilize society by maintaining the moral order. Shortly before contributing her name to the list of those supporting such views, Rossetti had published "A Helpmeet for Him," a poem that offers a similar view of womanhood:

> Woman was made for man's delight;
>  Charm, O woman, be not afraid!
> His shadow by day, his moon by night,
>  Woman was made.

12. "An Appeal Against Female Suffrage," *Nineteenth Century* 25 (June 1889): 782–83.
13. Ibid.

Her strength with weakness is overlaid;
Meek compliances veil her might;
Him she stays, by whom she is stayed.

World-wide champion of truth and right,
Hope in gloom and in danger aid,
Tender and faithful, ruddy and white,
Woman was made.

(*CP*, 2:169)

Considering Rossetti's opposition to the image of Eve as evil temptress, it is not surprising that she should contribute to the nineteenth-century representation of woman as moral guide in times of danger. Furthermore, the association of woman with the subdued light of shadow and moon is consistent with Rossetti's belief that because of Eve's disobedience, certain limitations were placed on all women. Considering the political context of the poem, one might read it as Rossetti's own antisuffrage appeal to women based upon the Bible. Appropriately, Rossetti first published "A Helpmeet for Him" in the Anglican journal *New and Old*, which by 1888 had firmly established an antisuffrage position.[14] Nevertheless, a modern reader still might wonder how a poet who in her earlier poems had depicted men as lazy princes and cruel seducers could then, in 1888, tell a woman reader she was made for "man's delight."

I would like to begin to answer this question by first focusing on the title, a direct allusion to the creation of Eve: "And the Lord said, it is not good that the man should be alone; I will make him an help meet for him" (Gen. 2:18). For modern readers, Rossetti's title may well appear to focus only on the relationship between Adam and Eve. However, to many Victorians who shared Rossetti's faith, this particular text and especially the word "helpmeet" brought with it the whole story of woman's creation, fall, and, most important, her redemption. Repeatedly, it was argued that because of Eve's fall, woman was degraded from her rightful position as helpmeet to that of man's slave, and a slave she remained until Christ's coming. He restored woman to the position Eve first held, that

---

14. For an indication of the journal's position on female suffrage, see "Woman Rights," *New and Old* 3 (July 1875): 142–54.

of helpmeet. As fellow religious poet and essayist Dora Greenwell, phrased it, "To be man's help-meet is woman's true vocation: for this, in the happy garden, she was given to the First Adam; and to be this, no longer Man's drudge or his plaything, the coming of the Second Adam has restored her."[15] For many of Rossetti's readers, therefore, "help-meet" brought with it some measure of dignity and respect. Furthermore, while for many readers, "helpmeet" still carried the meaning of subordination to man, that subordination was seen as social, not spiritual. Keeping these positive associations in mind, we can better understand what drew Rossetti to use the biblical text "a helpmeet for him" as her title. It was a text associated with Eve's and, therefore, all womankind's redemption through Christ. Christ's love, not Adam's, had restored her: "As love of his Lord enabled St. Peter to tread the sea, so love of the same Lord sets weak woman immovable on the waves of this troublesome world, triumphantly erect, despite her own frailty, made not 'like unto a wheel,' amid all the changes and chances of this mortal life" (*FD*, 310).

Furthermore, within the Anglican Church, there was an important debate over what it meant for a woman to be man's helper. Some clergy-men, such as Burgon, argued that even though woman was not man's slave, that she was created to be "man's helper" indicated her inferiority; Genesis, moreover, along with the teaching of St. Paul, made it clear that woman was to be subject to man's rule. But others, such as C. J. H. Fletcher, writing in response to Burgon, argued that "helper" meant woman was man's needed complement and that therefore she should not be seen as inferior to him but rather as part of him: "Adam is drawn by love to Eve as to her who could supply a want in him; the two together form a unit."[16] Although this image of woman as a necessary part of man still subordinates the feminine sphere to the masculine, the emphasis on woman's submissiveness to man is replaced by an emphasis on man's need for her.

Fletcher's argument provides a useful context in which to place Ros-

15. Dora Greenwell, "Our Single Women," in *Essays* (London: Alexander Strahan, 1866), 8.

16. Burgon, *To Educate Young Women*, 15; C. J. H. Fletcher, "Woman's Equality with Man in Christ: A Sermon," March 19, 1871, quoted in *Women in English Religion, 1700–1925*, ed. Dale A. Johnson (New York: Edwin Mellen Press, 1983), 144.

setti's poem. Significantly, the only major revision Rossetti made in the poem before including it in her 1888 collection serves to underscore the image of woman as a necessary complement to man. Line 7 in the version published in *New and Old* reads: "Firm she stands tho' sometime dismayed." As one can see, Rossetti's alteration to "Him she stays, by whom she is stayed," while suggesting that man checks or restrains woman at the same time he supports her, also stresses that woman supports man, implying that without her he might fall. Furthermore, the biblical echoes serve to reinforce this image of woman as a provider of spiritual comfort. The shadow image of line 3 calls to mind Ps. 121: "The Lord is thy shade upon thy right hand. The sun shall not smite thee by day, nor the moon by night" (Ps. 121:5–6). To be man's shadow, therefore, does not mean that woman follows as a shadow but rather that she provides helpful shelter from harm. Moreover, in that role of protector, she can be associated with the Lord. In fact, Rossetti establishes a close association between the Deity and woman in her association of woman with "delight." In Proverbs, for example, Wisdom, personified as female, refers to itself as "daily [God's] delight" (8:30) and in Psalm 1, the Psalmist describes the godly man as one who finds "his delight in the law of the Lord" (1:2). Rossetti often uses the word "delight" when speaking of Christ. For example, in "Feast of the Annunciation," she asserts, "Jesus is the One Delight" (*CP*, 2:238). With these associations in mind, Rossetti's assertion that "woman was made for man's delight" becomes less reactionary to modern ears than it may first sound. Clearly, "A Helpmeet for Him," which argues for woman's social subordination, also celebrates woman's spiritual power.

This image of woman supporting her man and offering spiritual comfort does bring to mind numerous nineteenth-century images of woman as loving wife, such as George Elgar Hicks' *Woman's Mission: Companion to Manhood*, or Millais' *Peace Concluded*, or even his *Order of Release*. Yet while many Victorians might have read Rossetti's helpmeet in these terms, there is ample evidence that other readings were quite possible. First, although "helpmeet" and "helpmate" are often used as if their meanings were interchangeable, those familiar with the original Hebrew phrase *ezer neged*, translated in the King James version as the two separate words, *help* and *meet*, would have been sensitive to the distinction. To be "meet" for man means woman is suitable or appropriate for man, but it does not necessarily mean she is mated to him as a wife. Thus, the Anglican readers of *New and Old*, and perhaps even Rossetti's more general audience, would not necessarily have read "helpmeet" as a synonym for devoted wife.

By the 1870s, Anglican writers had already offered rather liberal interpretations of what it meant for Eve to be Adam's helpmeet, and for women to be men's helpmeets. For example, Charlotte Yonge, best known for her Anglo-Catholic novels, defines "helpmeet" in a very general way. In her essay "Womankind," she writes, "All I want to do is to define what I believe to be the safe and true aspect in which woman ought to regard herself—namely, as the help-meet of man; not necessarily of any individual man, but of the whole Body who Christ our Lord has left to be waited on as Himself. He is her Lord. He will find her work to do for Him." The same interpretation appears in the work of Reverend Littledale, the Anglican theologian who was a personal friend of Rossetti's. In a lengthy essay on women and religious education, while referring to women as "helpmates," he also firmly argues that marriage is secondary: Women will have duties to perform, but first those duties must be toward "God and society" and only "possibly [will a woman] have to discharge them for a husband."[17] Placing Rossetti's poem within the context of such arguments suggests that the "him" in the title can be read not only as a reference to Adam and therefore mankind, but also as a reference to Christ. Rossetti's message to her women readers, therefore, while conservative politically, need not be read as a repudiation of her earlier work so critical of the Victorian marriage market.

To further our understanding of how Rossetti's "A Helpmeet for Him" might have been interpreted by a Victorian female audience, I will compare it to similar texts: Browning's "A Drama of Exile" and Jean Ingelow's "Remonstrance." The relevance of such comparisons was suggested to me first by the fact that Littledale not only concludes his essay with a quotation from Browning's poem but also presents the lines in such a way that they appear to be delivered by Browning herself to Victorian women. Moreover, that one could find in the Victorian market-

17. Charlotte Yonge, *Womankind* (London: Mozley and Smith, 1877), 4–5; Richard Frederick Littledale, "The Religious Education of Women," *Contemporary Review* 20 (June 1872): 24.

place anthologies of poems by women, seemingly published with a female audience in mind, such as *Home Thoughts and Home Scenes* (1865), suggests that woman's poetry did play a significant role in shaping female attitudes toward woman's mission. Ingelow's poem, which first appeared in her 1867 volume, was later included, under the title "Daughters of Eve" in *Queen's Gardens* (1888), another collection of women's verse aimed at a female audience.

Furthermore, I have chosen to focus on Browning and Ingelow in this comparison because during Rossetti's poetic career, they were both, in a sense, her rivals. Rossetti well might have imagined her verse being set against theirs, and even if she did not, reviewers often read her verse with either Browning or Ingelow in mind. In fact, although Browning died in 1861, a year before Rossetti's first volume was even published, by the 1880s it was a critical commonplace to set Browning and Rossetti against each other. Rossetti's major contemporary rival—in the marketplace, that is—was Ingelow. Although she did not achieve the critical status of either Rossetti or Browning, by the 1880s Ingelow had considerable popular success. (Available evidence suggests that she sold more copies of her poems than did Rossetti.)[18] In setting Rossetti next to these two other women poets, I am not claiming to do justice to either Browning's views on womanhood or Ingelow's; rather, I hope to demonstrate how Rossetti's "A Helpmeet for Him" functions within the Victorian debate on woman's mission, especially as that message was heard as being delivered by women to women.

Rossetti's poem, with its association of womanhood with "hope" and "aid," can be compared to Browning's representation of Eve in "A Drama of Exile." Especially relevant are those lines in which, on Christ's command, Adam blesses Eve, who is apparently kneeling overcome by grief, sorrow, and shame:

> Henceforward, rise, aspire
> To all the calms and magnaminities,

18. For evidence of the Victorian critic's tendency to judge Rossetti's work with Browning's in mind, see "Our Camp in the Woodland: A Day with the Gentle Poets," *Fraser's* 70 (August 1863): 204–13; and "Poetesses," *Saturday Review,* May 23, 1868, 678–79. For information on how well Ingelow's books sold, see Maureen Peters, *Jean Ingelow: Victorian Poetess* (Totowa, N.J.: Rowman and Littlefield, 1972), 64.

The lofty uses and the noble ends,
The sanctified devotion and full work
To which thou are elect for evermore,
First woman, wife, and mother!
. . . . . . . . . . . . . .
                    Rise, woman, rise
To thy peculiar and best altitudes
Of doing good and of enduring ill,
Of comforting for ill, and teaching good,
And reconciling all that ill and good
Unto the patience of a constant hope,—
Rise with thy daughters![19]

Both Rossetti and Browning seem in general agreement in regard to woman's mission to help others. Yet Rossetti's "helpmeet" as "shadow" and "moon" appears to have been assigned a less active role than Browning's Eve, who is being called to "full work" in the world. (In "A Drama of Exile," Browning's Eve steps first, before Adam, into the world of exile.)[20] One might conclude that Rossetti's image of womanhood is more passive than Browning's. However, the sound and rhythm of Rossetti's poem convey a sense of forward movement that contradicts such a message of passivity. The answer to this seeming contradiction lies in the fact that in "A Helpmeet for Him" there are really two images of womanhood: "Her strength with weakness is overlaid / Meek compliances veil her might." Weakness and compliance are only what appear on the surface; something of more substance and power stands behind the veil.

Both Browning and Rossetti offer women readers a text that seeks to empower them. The difference is in the perspective: Browning is focused on this world of work, while Rossetti, as is characteristic of her poetry, is looking beyond time to eternity. For Rossetti, the veil cast over woman's "might" would not be fully drawn back until time passed away.

19. *The Complete Works of Elizabeth Barrett Browning,* ed. Charlotte Porter and Helen A. Clarke, 6 vols. (1900; rpr., New York: AMS Press, 1973), 2:211–12.

20. For a more detailed analysis of Browning's Eve, see Marjorie Stone, *Elizabeth Barrett Browning* (New York: St. Martin's Press, 1995), 77–84; and Linda M. Lewis, "'Schooled by Sin': Reclaiming Eve in Elizabeth Barrett Browning's *A Drama of Exile,*" *Victorians Institute Journal* 22 (1994): 1–14.

Her commentary on the figure in Revelation of the woman "clothed with the sun" makes that point quite clear. Only after Christ's Second Coming would women be made "equal with men and angels." And then the helpmeet of Genesis could move "from the lowest place" to "the higher," becoming the woman of Revelation, the woman clothed with the sun (FD, 310). Although "A Helpmeet for Him" offers no explicit mention of that time of transformation, Rossetti's description of the helpmeet as "ruddy and white," an allusion to the Song of Songs (5:10), invites thoughts of the mystical union when, as the bride of Christ, the soul actually becomes Christlike, taking on Christ's image. Significantly, in Rossetti's poem "Christmas Day," she refers to the Christ child as "white and ruddy."

Where Browning's Eve is a figure serving to call women to noble work in the world, Rossetti's helpmeet is an image of transcendence, which not only urges women to participate in the world as providers of comfort and aid but also serves as a reminder of their spiritual power, suggesting a time and place beyond the world of exile. Turning to Ingelow's "Remonstrance" furthers our understanding of the place of "A Helpmeet for Him" in the Victorian canon of woman's poetry on womanhood.

Whereas Rossetti's speaker seeks to comfort and inspire women, ("Charm, O Woman, be not afraid"), Ingelow reprimands them: "Daughters of Eve! your mother did not well: / She laid the apple in our father's hand."[21] After firmly placing the blame for the fall of humankind on Eve, Ingelow's speaker continues to reinforce the notion of woman's inferiority, which lies behind such an interpretation of Genesis: "Daughters of Eve! he did not fall so far, as that sweet woman fell." Adam's decision to eat the apple is presented as a heroic act of self-sacrifice, and thus the speaker concludes, "For this, till love be reckoned less than lore, / Shall man be first and best for evermore." The only hope and comfort offered the daughters of Eve is not, as in Browning, meaningful work and not, as in Rossetti, spiritual transcendence, but marriage:

But God's great pity touched the grand mistake,
    And made his married love a sacred thing:

21. Jean Ingelow, "Remonstrance," *A Story of Doom and Other Poems* (Boston: Roberts Brothers, 1867), 232. All quotations from this poem are taken from this edition.

For yet his nobler sons, if aught be true,
Find the lost Eden in their love of you.

(232)

In these concluding lines, some elevation of woman's lower-class status can be found in Ingelow's association of married love with the sacred. However, the emphasis on marriage reinforces the conventional Victorian message to women that marriage is their highest goal, and the hope offered in these lines does little to counter the overall impression that Ingelow is reprimanding her female readers for entertaining any thoughts of equality with men, whether in this world or the next. With Ingelow's poem in mind, we can see that Rossetti's "A Helpmeet for Him" is not as conservative for its time as it may first appear. Certainly, Rossetti offers Victorian daughters of Eve a more celebratory vision of the feminine sphere than does Ingelow's "Remonstrance," which so clearly affirms the masculine.

As the previous chapters have shown, Rossetti did not participate in the idealization of manhood or the masculine. Not surprisingly, although Rossetti ultimately accepted woman's social subordination as the burden placed on all women by Eve's sin, she did not overlook the verse in Gen. 13:12 in which Adam seems quite willing to let Eve take all the blame: "The meanness as well as the heinousness of sin is illustrated in Adam's apparent effort to shelter himself at the expense of Eve" (*LS*, 84). Furthermore, while accepting woman's supporting role in society, she also reveals her fear that women will suffer in that role as man's helper:

Society may be personified as a human figure whose right hand is man whose left woman; in one sense equal, in another sense unequal. The right hand is labourer, acquirer, achiever: the left hand helps, but has little independence, and is more apt at carrying than at executing. The right hand runs the risks, fights the battles; the left hand abides in comparative quiet and safety; except (a material exception) that in the mutual relations of the twain it is in some ways far more liable to undergo than to inflict hurt, to be cut (for instance) than to cut. Rules admit of and are proved by exceptions. There are left-handed people and there may arise a lefthanded society! (*FD*, 410)

This left-handed society is presented as a passing thought, one Rossetti does not pursue. In fact, in *The Face of the Deep*, it is immediately followed by "'Do this, and he doeth it,'" her poem stressing acceptance of place. Yet mention of a left-handed society reveals her sympathy with those whose place was to serve in the passive role, and though she does not advocate a society ruled by women, her poem does give rise to thoughts of a society in which feminine characteristics are valued.

At one point in *Seek and Find*, Rossetti comforts women readers by comparing Christ's life of humility and sacrifice to woman's lot:

> In many points the feminine lot copies very closely the voluntarily assumed position of our Lord and Pattern. Woman must obey: and Christ "learned obedience" (Gen. iii.16; Heb. v. 8). She must be fruitful, but in sorrow: and He, symbolised by a corn of wheat, had not brought forth much fruit except He had died (Gen. iii.16; John xii.24). She by natural constitution is adapted not to assert herself, but to be subordinate: and He came not to be ministered unto but to minister; He was among His own "as he that serveth" (1 St. Peter iii 7; 1 Tim. ii.11, 12; St Mark x. 45; St. Luke xxii, 17). Her office is to be man's helpmeet: and concerning Christ God saith, "I have laid help upon One that is mighty" (Gen. ii. 18, 21, 22; Ps. lxxxix. 19). And well may she glory, in as much as one of the tenderest of divine promises takes (so to say) the feminine form: "As one whom his mother comforteth, so will I comfort you" (Is. lxvi.13). (30–31)

This passage echoes those clergymen of Rossetti's time who spoke of the "character of God" as a "mingling" of the masculine and feminine, and those who argued that Jesus Christ restored woman to her position of dignity not by being born of a woman, but by manifesting "womanly virtues."[22] Thus Rossetti should not be seen as standing alone against those who would see God only in masculine terms. Nor should we overlook her remarks on Christ's feminine character, which conclude with a

22. See H.W.C., "The Position of Woman," *English Woman's Journal* 6 (January 1861): 289; and Fletcher, "Woman's Equality with Man in Christ," quoted in *Women in English Religion*, ed. Johnson, 144.

reminder of woman's place: "But if our proud waves will after all not be stayed, or at any rate not be allayed (for stayed they must be) by the limit of God's ordinance concerning our sex, one final consolation yet remains to careful and troubled hearts: in Christ there is neither male nor female, for we are all one (Ga. iii. 28)" (*SF*, 30–32). Yet Rossetti's willingness to see the feminine in Christ sets her in opposition to the more popular "muscular Christianity" of her day, reminding us again that although conservative politically, Rossetti was often, for her time, radical in her religious thought.[23]

Rossetti's willingness to see the feminine aspect of Christ's life leads naturally to a more detailed consideration of her views on the Virgin Mary. For even though many Christians have viewed the mother of Jesus as merely a mediator between sinful human nature and the divine, some have gone so far as to see her as co-redeemer with Christ, and others have argued that she represents the feminine aspect of the Deity itself.[24] For Rossetti, Mary as the mother of Jesus was indeed set apart from other women. "Contemplating in her the glowing rose of motherhood grafted onto the lily of intact purity," Rossetti accepted the doctrine of Mary's perpetual virginity (*CS*, 181). Yet, Rossetti firmly rejected any line of thought that might lead to or even suggest the deification of the Virgin Mary. In her discussion of the Annunciation in *Called to Be Saints*, while associating Mary's soul with the dove, "the sweet symbol of tenderness," she nevertheless reminds the reader that "Mary is a shut gate, not a gate of access; Christ is our open door" (179, 181). Not surprisingly, the place of Mary within Roman Catholicism was seen by Rossetti as encouraging the worship of the creature before the Creator, and while, according to William Sharp, she "had much sympathy with the Church of Rome," she saw "Mariolatry" as its "most cardinal error."[25]

23. For a discussion of muscular Christianity and its popularity, see Norman Vance, *The Sinews of the Spirit: The Ideal of Christian Manliness in Victorian Literature and Religious Thought* (Cambridge: Cambridge University Press, 1985); and Donald E. Hall, ed., *Muscular Christianity: Embodying the Victorian Age* (Cambridge: Cambridge University Press, 1994).

24. For more detailed information on Mary's role in the Christian Church, see Marina Warner, *Alone of All Her Sex: The Myth and Cult of the Virgin Mary* (New York: Alfred A. Knopf, 1976); and Rosemary Radford Reuther, *Mary—The Feminine Face of the Church* (Philadelphia: Westminster Press, 1977).

25. William Sharp, "Some Reminiscences of Christina Rossetti," *Atlantic Monthly* 75 (June 1895): 745.

Yet Rossetti did find in the concept of motherhood a closeness to the divine. In a letter to her friend Caroline Gemmer she wrote, "The Maternal type is to me one of the dear & beautiful things which on earth helps us towards realizing that Archetype which is beyond all conception dear and beautiful. Mother's love patient, forgiving, all-outlasting, cannot but be the copy & pledge of Love all-transcending."[26] While Rossetti's religious poetry more often draws on the bride and bridegroom imagery in depicting the soul's relationship to the divine, she does occasionally portray God in maternal terms. For example, in "After This the Judgment," the weary and frightened soul pleads, "Love me as very mother loves her son, / Her sucking firstborn fondled on her knee" (CP, 1:185). How did Rossetti come to this vision of the maternal divine if she resisted worshiping the mother of Jesus?

Speaking of God as a mother was not typical of Victorian religious discourse; however, certainly Rossetti was aware, as these lines in her poem suggest (and as does the reference to Isa. 16:13 in her discussion of Christ's feminine traits), that the image of a maternal deity can be found in the Bible, especially in the Old Testament. She also may have been familiar with the writings of female medieval mystics in which Christ is at times imagined as a female parent.[27] Furthermore, the deification of motherhood was very much a part of Victorian culture. As Kathleen Hickok notes, "The sanctification of motherhood occurs in poem after poem, by women as well as men, in the nineteenth century."[28] Yet more influential than any biblical imagery, mystical writing, or cultural characteristic was the presence of Rossetti's own mother. If one recalls Rossetti's image of Eve standing before God's throne, the image with which this chapter began, one realizes that there is actually a fourth feminine image that informs Rossetti's interpretation of both the feminine and the spiritual—her "own immediate dear mother" (FD, 310). Before concluding this examination of Rossetti's views on Eve and the woman

---

26. Christina G. Rossetti to Caroline Gemmer, [January 26, 1875], quoted in Antony H. Harrison, "Christina Rossetti and Caroline Gemmer: Friendship by Royal Mail," *Victorians Institute Journal* 24 (1996): 239.

27. Colleen Hobbs makes this point in her article "A View from 'The Lowest Place': Christina Rossetti's Devotional Prose," *Victorian Poetry* 32 (autumn–winter 1994): 416.

28. Kathleen Hickok, *Representations of Women: Nineteenth-Century British Women's Poetry* (Westport, Conn.: Greenwood Press, 1984), 89.

question, we should therefore consider the role Rossetti's mother played in shaping her beliefs. As was typical for the time, Rossetti was educated at home and by her mother. Moreover, as Rossetti's biographer Frances Thomas points out, Rossetti's father allowed his wife "to direct all matters of religion."[29] Thus we can assume that her mother first introduced Rossetti to Christianity. Here it is important to recall that Rossetti did not see the biological fact of motherhood as essential in defining the maternal type. In Rossetti's eyes, a genuine "nursing mother" was a woman who, in a sense, fed others with the words of God or who nurtured those who would (*FD*, 312; *SF*, 129). All biographers agree that Frances Rossetti fulfilled this role both by what she said and how she lived. The fact that Rossetti learned her faith from her mother must be seen as a significant element in Rossetti's ability to imagine Eve as redeemed woman and to resist, at least to some extent, misogynist views of womanhood.

Evidence of the important role Rossetti's mother played in her spiritual life can be found in her poetry. The dedicatory sonnet in *A Pageant and Other Poems* offers an image that depicts Frances Rossetti as the first teacher of love and one who still serves as guide:

> Sonnets are full of love, and this my tome
> Has many sonnets: so here now shall be
> One sonnet more, a love sonnet, from me
> To her whose heart is my heart's quiet home,
> To my first Love, my Mother, on whose knee
> I learned love-lore that is not troublesome;
> Whose service is my special dignity,
> And she my loadstar while I go and come.

> (*CP*, 2:59)

The series of Valentine poems Rossetti wrote for her mother, one for each year beginning in 1876 and ending in 1886, the year of her mother's death, offers further proof of Mrs. Rossetti's importance in her daughter's spiritual life. In her 1884 Valentine poem, for example, Rossetti echoes

29. Frances Thomas, *Christina Rossetti* (Hanley Swan, Eng.: Self-Publishing Association, 1992), 42.

slightly her own famous "Up-hill." This time, however, she imagines the difficult up-hill journey being made easier by a mother who shows her the way: "bless me still, O Mother mine, / While hand in hand we scale life's hill, / You Guide, & I your Valentine" (*CP,* 3:317). Rossetti's most moving tribute to her mother, and her sister, who also served as a maternal figure, is the following untitled sonnet, written at some point after Mrs. Rossetti's death, in which paradise, the world after death and before the Resurrection, is imagined as a place of mothers and sisters:

Our Mothers, lovely women pitiful;
    Our Sisters, gracious in their life and death;
    To us each unforgotten memory saith:
"Learn as we learned in life's sufficient school,
Work as we worked in patience of our rule,
    Walk as we walked, much less by sight than faith,
    Hope as we hoped, despite our slips and scathe,
Fearful in joy and confident in dule."
I know not if they see us or can see;
    But if they see us in our painful day,
      How looking back to earth from Paradise
      Do tears not gather in those loving eyes?—
    Ah, happy eyes! whose tears are wiped away
Whether or not you bear to look on me.

                    (*CP,* 2:292)

The pronoun change from "us" to "me" in the last line renders the poem an especially personal expression of longing for both the peace of paradise and maternal love and recognition. The last line becomes almost confessional in that the speaker appears to feel distanced not only by death but by her own unworthiness. Yet in this last line there is also the echo of a prayer that these "lovely" and "gracious" women "look on" her, in other words, that they recognize her with concern and pity in their eyes. If they do so, she might be able to follow, to "walk as [they] walked" and thus join them in paradise.

How Rossetti's love for her mother is viewed, of course, varies with the time. For example, although all biographers agree that there are no signs of resentment on Rossetti's part toward her mother, early commentators tend to depict the years Rossetti spent as her mother's companion as a sign of praiseworthy devotion, whereas more recent critics and biographers occasionally suggest complex motives and costs.[30] And, of course, it is important to remember that in Victorian society a daughter, especially an unmarried daughter, would have been expected to care for her elderly parents. Whatever Rossetti's motivation for serving as the devoted daughter, her relationship with her mother became central to her understanding of woman's spiritual life and to Rossetti's appreciation of the feminine sphere. This becomes especially clear when one examines the original place of publication of this sonnet of faith, love, and grief. This poem appears appropriately in the "New Jerusalem and Its Citizens" section of *Verses* (1893), but Rossetti first published "Our Mothers lovely women pitiful" in *The Face of the Deep*, placing it immediately after her discussion of the Whore of Babylon and the Strange Woman, the figures Rossetti saw as conveying a special warning for women, a warning against rebelliousness and disobedience. Read in this context, the poem seems offered by Rossetti as a contrasting point serving as a response to these destructive images of the feminine. It is as if Rossetti is providing her readers, especially her female readers, with an example of women whose steps lead to heaven, not hell, so as to give all daughters of Eve hope.

To modern eyes, Rossetti's faith, which prevented her from supporting woman's suffrage, may well appear repressive; however, Rossetti found comfort, strength, and meaning in her religion. She accepted her role as helpmeet, as a left hand in a right-handed society, and in "A Helpmeet for Him" she urged other women to do so as well. Yet because of that faith, she was also able to contribute to a decidedly positive construction of the feminine. She was able to regard Eve not as evil temptress in a fallen garden but as a beloved mother before God's throne.

Even though Rossetti seems to have often seen herself in terms of daughter, and at times a weak daughter needing the comfort and help of

---

30. See, for example, Dolores Rosenblum, *Christina Rossetti: The Poetry of Endurance* (Carbondale, Ill.: Southern Illinois University Press, 1986), 147; and Thomas, *Christina Rossetti*, 112. Rosenblum offers a Freudian reading of the mother-daughter relationship, arguing that Rossetti experienced an Oedipal conflict with her mother. Thomas suggests that perhaps having such a perfect mother made Rossetti "more aware of her own inferiority."

a loving mother, she herself was seen by others as a spiritual guide in the difficult journey uphill. Through both her poetry and her devotional prose, Rossetti became an especially important religious voice in the last years of the nineteenth century. Rossetti never totally rejected what St. Paul writes in 1 Tim. 2:11–12 regarding the silencing of women; she found a way, however, to qualify it by using his words from 2 Tim. 1:5, words that praise other women of faith, like herself: "St. Paul has written: 'Let the woman learn in silence with all subjection. But I suffer not a woman to teach.' Yet elsewhere he wrote: 'I call to remembrance the unfeigned faith . . . which dwelt first in thy grandmother Lois, and thy mother Eunice'" (FD, 195). By turning to her biblical foremothers who had believed in Christ, Rossetti finds a way to justify the fact that in six books of devotional prose and in hundreds of religious poems, she speaks to others of her faith and in so doing assumes the role of a spiritual teacher.

*six*

# DARING TO SPEAK TO OTHERS
## Rossetti as a Religious Poet

✝

IT IS A COMMONPLACE OF NINETEENTH-CENTURY SCHOLARSHIP that the Victorian Age was one of religious doubt. For example, in his recent work on the subject, Lance St. John Butler sees the midpoint of the age, 1870, as an especially significant date; then, he argues, the Victorian discourse concerning religion "shifted to give preponderance to doubt."[1] Rossetti resisted this shift entirely. Indeed, during this time, her vocational life and spiritual life blended completely, and she became predominantly a religious writer. All her devotional prose was written after 1870, as was most of her religious poetry. That Rossetti not only continued to believe during a time of increased religious doubt but also made that belief the major burden of her poetry was an important factor in her critical reception during these years. As one reviewer of *Verses*, Rossetti's 1893 volume of devotional poetry, phrased it: "'The voice of one crying in the wilderness': that is Miss Rossetti's poetry in our arid days. . . . Almost alone among English poets Miss Rossetti keeps aloft the Standard of Christ—keeps it flying with an undaunted hope." Another critic, when evaluating the significance of her "message," favored her poetry over

---

1. Lance St. John Butler, *Victorian Doubt: Literary and Cultural Discourses* (New York: Harvester, 1990), 86; see also Walter E. Houghton, *The Victorian Frame of Mind, 1830–1870* (New Haven: Yale University Press, 1957), 18–22.

that of William Morris and Algernon Swinburne because, he concluded, "Miss Rossetti yields place to [their] dismal negations not for a moment." Even the theologian and Bible critic, B. F. Westcott, the bishop of Durham at the time of Rossetti's death, wrote at length about her "spiritual teaching" and found her message especially needed in what he saw as a materialistic age.[2]

While religion certainly functioned during the nineteenth century as a means of social control over women's behavior, it is important to recognize that many men, even Anglican bishops, were willing to listen to a religious writer who was a woman.[3] Rossetti's devotional reading diary, *Time Flies*, sold seven thousand copies; *The Face of the Deep*, her commentary on the Apocalypse, went through six editions; and by 1912, twenty-one thousand copies of *Verses* had been printed.[4] Sales figures on her other devotional works are difficult to obtain, but we do know that *Seek and Find* was still being published in 1906 and *Called to Be Saints* in 1912. Certainly, both women and men were buying and reading these works. Possibly, Anglican vicars read Rossetti and occasionally drew upon her teaching for their sermons; furthermore, Rossetti's devotional poetry and prose appears to have been well received by members of the Methodist Church as well.[5] Clearly, Rossetti's faith gave her a place from which to speak to others, and members of both sexes sometimes listened.

Thus, rather than focus on how Rossetti's faith limited her creative life, as several critics have done, I will consider how her spiritual life enriched it. First, not only did her faith inspire almost all of her later poetry, but that faith, which Rossetti held during a time of religious doubt, also contributed to developing in her a strong sense of purpose and audience.

2. "Miss Rossetti's *Verses*," *Speaker*, November 25, 1893, 588; A. Smellie, "Christina Rossetti and Her Message," *Wesleyan Methodist Magazine* 118 (1895): 206; B. F. Westcott, *An Appreciation of the Late Christina Georgina Rossetti* (London: Society for Promoting Christian Knowledge, 1899), 21, 22.

3. For a discussion of religion as a social control over Victorian women, see Judith Rowbotham, *Good Girls Make Good Wives* (Oxford: Basil Blackwell, 1989), 53–98.

4. W.K.L.C., Introduction to *Verses* by Christina Rossetti (London: Society for Promoting Christian Knowledge, 1925), 10.

5. My copy of *Time Flies* has written inside it "St. Luke's Vicarage, Newcastle-upon-Tyne," and the previous owner has made pencil marks throughout. See "Christina Rossetti's Devotional Prose," *Methodist Review* 80 (September 1898): 798–805, for evidence that members of the Methodist faith held her in high regard.

Rossetti's Christian faith told her that she was indeed her "brother's [and sister's] keeper" and that she must therefore write so as to help not hinder others in their journey toward God. Second, this increased sense of responsibility for the spiritual well-being of her readers contributed to the significant changes that occur in her later poetic voice, changes that Rossetti scholars have, as of yet, not fully recognized.

A tendency in Rossetti scholarship to ignore chronology when discussing her religious poetry has led to the view that both Rossetti's religious poetry and her spiritual experience remained more or less the same from her teenage years to her death.[6] Such an approach is problematic. In general, it overlooks the whole process of human maturation, and in Rossetti's case, it disregards the possibility that illness (in January 1872 Rossetti was diagnosed with Graves' disease) or grief (her sister died in 1876, her brother Dante Gabriel in 1882, and her mother in 1886) in any way influenced Rossetti's understanding of human spirituality. If one focuses on Rossetti's later poetry, that is, the poems in *A Pageant and Other Poems* (1881), and especially those first published in *Time Flies* and *The Face of the Deep*, one notices a distinct difference in Rossetti's religious message from that in her earlier poems. While vanity of vanities is still a theme that she employs, she quite clearly moves, during the 1880s, from echoing the message of Ecclesiastes to echoing the First Epistle of St. John. The Rossetti of these later poems is the spiritual poet and religious teacher the Victorians so admired. She was the poet who, in an age of religious doubt, kept singing that God is Love.

As this chapter will show, Rossetti's later poetry repeatedly echoes not only the message but often the very language of 1 John 4:7–12:

Beloved, let us love one another: for love is of God; and every one that loveth is born of God, and knoweth God. He that loveth not knoweth not God; for God is love. In this was manifested the love of God toward us, because that God sent his only begotten Son into the world, that we might live through him. Herein is love, not that we loved God, but that he loved us, and sent his Son to be the propitiation for our sins. Beloved, if God so loved us, we ought also to love one another.

6. See, for example, Dolores Rosenblum, "Christina Rossetti's Religious Poetry: Watching, Looking, Keeping Vigil," *Victorian Poetry* 20 (spring 1982): 33–49.

Before exploring Rossetti's poetic echoing of St. John, I will consider at least briefly what biblical scholars say about St. John's first epistle. A recent scholar, Judith M. Lieu, points out that "commentators old and new" have consistently seen "the theme of love" as the "heart" of this epistle, and of course, when using the word "love," biblical scholars are referring to the concept of *agape,* not *eros.*[7] They emphasize that John, especially in 4:7–12, links God's selfless love for humanity, shown in Christ, with the love human beings are to show for one another. As Lieu points out, through this theme of love, "John can speak of God's relationship with believers, believers' relationship with God and their relationship with one another."[8] That Rossetti should be drawn to such a text is significant. It suggests that as she matured spiritually, she was thinking as much of her relationship with other human beings (those other human beings would, of course, include her readers) as she was thinking of her relationship with God, for the two relationships would have been interdependent in her mind.

*A Pageant and Other Poems* includes several poems that speak of life in weary tones, such as "Soeur Louise" and "Fluttered Wings," in which the speaker appears focused on her relationship with God and unconcerned with her listeners. However, throughout the volume there are moments when a joyous, or at least comforting, love song (or speech) responds to a mournful silence. Rossetti first draws attention to this pattern in "The Key-Note," a lyric placed immediately after her dedicatory sonnet to her mother. Indeed, by placing this poem as the first in the table of contents and by titling it "The Key-Note," Rossetti suggests to her readers that all the poems that follow can be read as her commitment to continue singing in answer to the silence of winter. Although the speaker begins with a mournful lament, suggesting that both inspiration and joy are gone—"Where are the songs I used to know"—she concludes with a statement of hope:

7. Judith M. Lieu, *The Theology of the Johannine Epistles* (Cambridge: Cambridge University Press, 1991), 66. See also C. H. Dodd, *The Johannine Epistles* (New York: Harper and Brothers, 1946), 109–10, for a discussion of the meaning of *agape* as it is used throughout the New Testament.
8. Lieu, *Theology,* 66.

Yet Robin sings thro' Winter's rest,
  When bushes put their berries on;
  While they their ruddy jewels don,
He sings out of a ruddy breast;
  The hips and haws and ruddy breast
    Make one spot warm where snowflakes lie,
They break and cheer the unlovely rest
  Of Winter's pause— and why not I?

                      (*CP*, 2:59–60)

The initial world-weariness of the speaker does not lead to a desire for rest, as in some of Rossetti's early poems, but to a renewed sense of purpose. Finding in the robin's song and in the berried bush exemplary models, the speaker commits herself to affirming life even when the season of the year, and of one's life, is winter. Despite its melancholy first line, "The Key-Note" is about creativity and life, not loss and death. Moreover, it is a poem about love, for it tells of communicating with others so as to comfort and cheer: the robin and nature's red berries speak to the poet, and she in turn speaks to the reader of hope.

"The Key-Note" does not appear to be a religious poem and need not necessarily be read as addressing issues of the spiritual life. However, for one familiar with Rossetti's work, religious overtones can be heard, especially in the seasonal imagery. One need only recall the third lyric in Rossetti's "Old and New Year Ditties" ("Passing away, saith the world"), in which Rossetti echoes the Song of Songs 2:10–11, to recognize that in Rossetti's religious vocabulary, winter was a season associated with a time of waiting for Christ the bridegroom. Read in this context, "The Key-Note" suggests that Rossetti is encouraging her readers to find, even while one waits for spiritual fulfillment, reason to sing.

Significantly, in *A Pageant and Other Poems*, Rossetti does not explicitly distinguish between her general poems and her devotional poems; in other words, there is no separate section entitled "devotional," as in her previous two volumes. Furthermore, even though the volume does conclude with a collection of poems that directly addresses, especially in their use of biblical language, the soul's relationship to God, poems of an explicitly religious nature such as "Golden Silences" are also woven throughout the whole volume. In "Golden Silences," the speaker quite clearly employs a religious vocabulary and leads the reader to a contemplation of heaven, and again, as in "The Key-Note," Rossetti moves from silence to sound. The speaker begins with the silences of both sadness and death as her subject:

> There is a silence that saith, "Ah me!"
>     There is silence that nothing saith;
>         One the silence of life forlorn,
>     One the silence of death;
> One is, and the other shall be.

(CP, 2:106)

However, the poem ends with a firm prediction of a time when all silences shall end:

> Sowing day is a silent day,
>     Resting night is a silent night;
>         But whoso reaps the ripened corn
>     Shall shout in his delight,
> While silences vanish away.

(2:106)

Within a biblical framework, for those who have a spiritual harvest to reap, both the silence of sorrow and the silence of death shall end in shouts of heavenly joy.

It is appropriate to point out here that as Rossetti matured as a poet she was, not surprisingly, especially responsive to biblical texts that describe heaven as a place of song. For example, when commenting on Rev. 14:2–3 ("I heard the voice of harpers harping with their harps: And they sung as it were a new song before the Throne"), Rossetti writes: "Heaven is revealed to earth as the home-land of music: of music, thus remote from what is gross or carnal; exhibiting like-wise an incalculable range of variety, which rebukes and silences perverse suggestions of monotonous tedium in the final beatitude" (FD, 352). When meditating on Rev. 8:1, a text telling of a half-hour "silence in heaven," Rossetti concludes that such a silence occurs only because at this moment in St. John's vision, heaven "may have been looking or preparing to look earthwards" (241). For Rossetti, as "Golden Silences" suggests, silence was a characteristic of a fallen earth: "Silence seems unnatural, incongruous, in heaven. On this occasion [see Rev. 8:1] and remotely we may surmise it to be a result of the Fall, for when earth first saw the light in panoply of beauty the morning stars sang together and all the sons of God shouted for joy: sinless earth, for sinless it then seems to have been whether or not inhabited, called forth instead of silencing an outburst of celestial music" (*FD*, 241).

In "The Thread of Life," a meditative poem placed well within the grouping of religious poems that concludes *A Pageant and Other Poems*, Rossetti offers her readers what is perhaps her most powerful statement regarding her commitment to writing a poetry that would prefigure the "celestial music" of heaven. As with "Golden Silences" and "The Key-Note," this poem begins with the typical Rossettian tones of her early verse. "The Thread of Life" is a series of three sonnets, and in the first sonnet the speaker tells of a youthful and hopeful vision of life now lost:

> And sometimes I remember days of old
> When fellowship seemed not so far to seek
> And all the world and I seemed much less cold,
> And at the rainbow's foot lay surely gold,
> And hope felt strong and life itself not weak.
>
> (*CP*, 2:122)

These notes of regret and melancholy, however, are not sustained. In the third sonnet, the speaker gives herself to God, having recognized the meaning of Christ's loving sacrifice for her. And God's love, thus recognized, enables her to sing a "sweet new song":

> And this myself as king unto my King
> I give, to Him Who gave Himself for me;
> Who gives Himself to me, and bids me sing
> A sweet new song of His redeemed set free;
> He bids me sing: O death, where is thy sting?
> And sing: O grave, where is thy victory?
>
> (2:123)

She shall sing, not of loss and death, nor of silence and the inability to speak to others, but quite the opposite. Rossetti, echoing St. Paul (see 1 Cor. 15:55), tells her readers that she shall sing of divine love and its power over the silence of death. The "merrymaking crew" of the second sonnet in the series may, of course, not hear this song, but presumably the reader who holds a copy of *A Pageant and Other Poems* will.

Significantly, although one of the major pieces of this volume, *Monna Innominata*, ends with the unnamed lady alone in sorrowful silence, this sonnet sequence is answered within the context of *A Pageant* by a second sequence, *Later Life*. This second sequence functions, as Linda Schofield points out, "as a kind of rebuttal to the concerns" of the more secular sequence.[9] Whereas *Monna Innominata* focuses on the relationship between the female speaker, her beloved, and God, *Later Life* expands the concept of love from the individual and the personal level to the general. In other words, Rossetti explores the relationship between a speaker (the sex of the speaker remains unspecified), all other human beings (not just one beloved), and God. Moreover, although *Later Life* contains Sonnet 27, an anguished statement of the speaker's fear of death and damnation, Rossetti does not conclude with this thought of total isolation from love but rather with an image of all human beings united, living and dead:

> The dead may be around us, dear and dead;
>> The unforgotten dearest dead may be
>>> Watching us with unslumbering eyes and heart;
> Brimful of words which cannot yet be said,
>> Brimful of knowledge they may not impart,
>> Brimful of love for you and love for me.

(CP, 2:150)

In these last lines, Rossetti focuses the reader on a time when the love of the beloved dead will be expressed in a fullness that is unimaginable now. In the reference to "you" in the last line, the speaker reaches out from the text of the poem to include the reader in this community of love.

Appropriately, Rossetti concludes *A Pageant*, which, as I have tried to

<hr>

9. Linda Schofield, "Displaced and Absent Texts as Contexts for Christina Rossetti's *Monna Innominata*," *Journal of Pre-Raphaelite Studies*, n.s., 6 (spring 1997): 47.

show, periodically takes the reader from mournful silence to comforting if not joyous expression, with a dialogue of love between the fearful soul and God. The anguished soul speaks first, confessing: "I have not sought Thee, I have not found Thee, / I have not thirsted for Thee." This voice, which is overcome by fears of death, then asks for God's love: "Wilt Thou look upon, wilt Thou see / Thy perishing me?" Not only is God not silent, but the answer given concludes with an image of a final and complete union of love between the individual soul and the Deity:

"Yea, long ago with love's bands I bound thee:
Now the Everlasting Arms surround thee,—
   Thro' death's darkness I look and see
   And clasp thee to Me."

(2:164)

Thus, *A Pageant* draws to a close on a message of absolute love expressed by the voice of God.

Rossetti arranged both *Goblin Market* and *The Prince's Progress* so as to move the reader to a consideration of divine love, but there are indications that she feared she was, as a writer, often too melancholy. As early as 1863, in the letter to Dora Greenwell in which Rossetti refers to her early version of "The Prince's Progress" as a "reverse of the Sleeping Beauty," she reveals her concern that as a Christian she has not displayed the proper attitude: "I suppose except in fairy land such reverses must often occur; yet I don't think it argues a sound or grateful spirit to dwell on them predominantly as I have done." Rossetti's misgivings were perhaps reinforced by the occasional reviewer's comment. Though she did receive, on the whole, positive reviews throughout her career, she was at times taken to task for her lack of optimism. For example, regarding *Prince's Progress*, a critic for the *Athenaeum* wrote: "We notice, indeed, not without regret, that most of these poems are set in a minor key—that a strain of suffering insinuates itself even into the author's devotional pieces. . . . In the poetic mind, if in any, we expect this instinct [the spiritual instinct] to predominate; and we cannot but lament that the tone of Miss Rossetti's poetry—always be it remembered, religiously submissive—should be that of the dirge rather than of the anthem." And at least one critic of *A Pageant* complained that too many poems in the volume were pessimistic: Some of the sonnets and lyrics "outdo in dark misgivings, and in suggestions of death, all that Miss Rossetti has heretofore written. . . . She has consulted her sense of loss and her weakness too much, and the healthy imagination too little."[10]

That Rossetti well may have been troubled by such a response to her work is suggested not only by a personal letter to Greenwell but also by two entries in *Time Flies*. For January 2, she offers her readers the following thought: "A certain masterly translator has remarked that whatever may or may not constitute a good translation it cannot consist in turning a good poem into a bad one. This suggestive remark opens to investigation a world-wide field. Thus, for instance, he (or she) cannot be an efficient Christian who exhibits the religion of love as unlovely" (*TF*, 2). This concern over how one's life and work is read by others is further developed in a lengthy meditation on gloomy Christians, which she offers her readers as the entry for May 29:

A gloomy Christian is like a cloud before the rainbow was vouchsafed.

We all (or almost all) more or less present cloudy aspects, thanks to tempers, griefs, anxieties, disappointments.

But the heavenliest sort of Christian exhibits more bow than cloud, walking the world in a continual thanksgiving; and "a joyful and pleasant thing it is to be thankful."

At unequal distances behind and below him tramp on graduated Christians of every density and tinge: some with full-coloured bows, some with a faint bit of broken bow, some with the merest tint of prismatic colour at a torn edge; all bearing some sign of God's gracious covenant with them.

In this company we fail to trace the gloomy Christian, all cloud, no bow.

But if he really and truly is not traceable high or low among the

10. Rossetti to Dora Greenwell, [October 1863], *The Collected Letters of Christina Rossetti*, ed. Antony H. Harrison, 4 vols. (Charlottesville: University of Virginia Press, 1997), 1:184; review of *The Prince's Progress and Other Poems*, *Athenaeum*, June 23, 1866, 825; review of *A Pageant and Other Poems*, *British Quarterly Review* 147 (October 1881): 248.

caravan of pilgrims with their badge of hope, where is he to be sought for on holy ground? (102)

The last line of this entry serves almost as a warning to both Rossetti's readers and herself. Clearly, by the time she published *Time Flies,* she had decided that she must be careful as a poet not to exhibit Christianity to her readers as if it were an unlovely religion of gloom. As G. B. Tennyson discusses in his work on Victorian devotional poetry, Rossetti's "very approach to poetry" became tightly interwoven with her faith, for writing poetry for her was a "way of seeking the Deity"; in other words, writing poetry was a form of prayer.[11] I would also like to emphasize that for Rossetti, poetry became an important way of fulfilling her duty to others. In *Time Flies,* when commenting on the bishop's pastoral staff, she concludes: "For my own behoof therefore I wind up by reflecting that every Christian is constituted 'king and priest' [see Rev. 1:6] in our Father's kingdom: that in consequence some grade of pastoral work devolves on each of us, if not as a dignity yet as a responsibility: and that as regards every soul within reach of our influence we all are in truth our 'brother's keeper'" (123). In *The Face of the Deep,* she repeats this point: "Our gifts, talents, opportunities, are a trust vested in us for the definite purpose of glorifying God, benefitting man, working out our own salvation. Ours are,—then mine are" (275).

As Rossetti worked out her salvation, it is quite possible that she came to feel that writing poems of world-weariness and of love lost, even if those themes were interwoven with a message of the spiritual life to follow death, did not benefit her readers. Not surprisingly, therefore, the pattern of silence and sorrow answered by song and joy, which is woven throughout *A Pageant* becomes in *Time Flies,* published four years later, a major organizing principle. When Rossetti places a poem for daily reading in *Time Flies,* any tones of world-weariness are immediately answered by a message of hope. For example, the first poem in the volume, "A heavy heart, if ever heart was heavy," concludes on a note of affirmation. Once the speaker lifts her heart to Christ, she is no longer weighed down with sorrow, and the tone of the poem shifts dramatically:

11. G. B. Tennyson, *Victorian Devotional Poetry: The Tractarian Mode* (Cambridge: Harvard University Press, 1981), 202.

Lifted to Thee my heart weighs not so heavy,
  It leaps and lightens lifted up to Thee;
It sings, it hopes to sing amid the bevy
    Of thousand thousand choirs that sing, and see
  Thy Face, me loving, for Thou lovest me.

                             (CP, 2:305)

A similar movement from weariness and regret to anticipation and joy occurs in the poem beginning "When sick of life and all the world." And in several other poems in the volume, Rossetti assumes the voice of one who urges those who feel weary to endure, as in the poem beginning "Through burden and heat of the day," or the poem that opens with the question "Have dead men long to wait?" and the sonnet beginning, "Is any grieved or tired?" (As is typical of many of Rossetti's later religious poems, none of these poems are titled.)

Moreover, when Rossetti includes a poem that dwells on the speaker's sorrow, she makes it part of a series, even numbering each poem in the series so as to emphasize that any sorrow or lament is only part of a larger whole. For example, the poem placed as the reading for February 11, which bears the biblical epigraph, "I see that all things come to an end," is followed by the poem bearing as its epigraph the second part of that biblical text: "But Thy Commandment is exceeding broad." (See Ps. 119:96, Book of Common Prayer version.) Whereas the first poem tells of the time when even the "ocean's roar" shall be silenced, the second, placed as the reading for February 12, urges the reader to "rouse thy soul" and "hope afresh, for hope shall not be vain" (CP, 2:311). The entries for October 4 and 5 work in much the same way. First, echoing the biblical text Mic. 1:8, the speaker tells how she has been acting like a "mournful owl" and "doleful dragon." In the second sonnet in the series, however, that placed for October 5, she associates herself with all the voices which respond to the joyous song of the lark:

These [voices] set me singing too at unawares:
  One note for all delights and charities,
    One note for hope reviving with the light,
  One note for every lovely thing that is;

Till while I sang my heart cast off its cares
And revelled in the land of no more night.

(2:326)

The phrase "every lovely thing" echoes slightly St. Paul's letter to the
Philippians (see Phil. 4:8) in which he tells his audience to think on
things that are "lovely" and of "good report." And in Rossetti's religious
vocabulary, the "land of no more night" is, of course, heaven.

Since *Time Flies* is in many ways a personal document, one in which
Rossetti often speaks in the first person and relates personal experiences
in the prose meditations, a reader is strongly inclined to interpret the
speaker of the poems as Rossetti herself. Thus when, in the last poem
before the appendix, one placed as part of the December 31 entry, the
reader hears a voice reflecting on the past and finding that in later life all
is harmonized, one is inclined to read this poem as Rossetti's reflections
on her spiritual and poetic life.

Looking back along life's trodden way
    Gleams and greenness linger on the track;
Distance melts and mellows all today,
    Looking back.

Rose and purple and a silvery grey,
    Is that cloud the cloud we called so black?
Evening harmonizes all today,
    Looking back.

Foolish feet so prone to halt or stray,
    Foolish heart so restive on the rack!
Yesterday we sighed, but not today
    Looking back.

(CP, 2:335)

With *Time Flies*, Rossetti fully enters a new phase in her poetic career. In
thinking of her responsibility as a Christian, she answers her earlier la-
ments over life's vanity and her "restive heart"; she becomes a poet who
not only sighs, longing for God, but also one who sings, both accepting

159

the pattern of her life as God's will and looking forward to the joy of heaven.

Furthermore, she seeks to include the reader in that experience of acceptance and joy. Significantly, in the entry for December 31, Rossetti uses the pronoun "we," not I. In other words, Rossetti's poetry becomes, in a sense, less personal. By that I mean that even though the poetry is presented in both *Time Flies* and *The Face of the Deep* as if it were indeed her own voice, and not a persona distinct from the poet, nevertheless it is a voice that could be interpreted as belonging to every or any human being who seeks God. As Rossetti matured, she was attempting to change the poetic voice of her religious poems so that it might represent not just the personal expression of one soul but also that of her audience, especially those Christian readers who would buy *Time Flies*, seeking spiritual solace and guidance. Looking closely at three other poems first published in *Time Flies* will help make this point.

"Better So," composed 1861, was never published, but a shorter version appears in *Time Flies* for July 23. This published version has no title; it simply begins with the question: "Who would wish back the Saints upon our rough / Wearisome road?" In "Better So," the speaker has one "familiar friend" in mind. The earlier version is thus very much an expression of a personal grief. In the published version, the one familiar friend becomes simply "one": "I would not fetch one back to hope with me / A hope deferred" (*CP*, 2:309). Thus the poem included in *Time Flies* is applicable to a wider audience. It does not apply to just one particular person who has lost a beloved but to all those who grieve.

More striking are the differences between "'The Heart Knoweth Its Own Bitterness,'" composed in 1857, and a much altered later version entitled "'Whatsoever is right, that shall ye receive,'" which Rossetti places as the reading for August 17. The change in the biblical text, from Prov. 14:10 to Matt. 20:7, used as the title points to the significant change in meaning in the revision process. Rather than speak about the self, the revised version speaks to others. Rossetti accomplishes such a transformation by taking from the original version only the first and last stanzas, and by making slight but significant changes in these two stanzas.

By choosing to keep only two of the original stanzas, Rossetti transforms the tone so that the anger and disappointment, the "bitterness" expressed in the first version is totally removed. Thus, "'Whatsoever is right'" has no mention of those human beings who cannot fulfill or satisfy the speaker, as does the original. Rather, it is a comforting statement of faith and trust in God:

> When all the overwork of life
>     Is finished once, and fallen asleep
> We shrink no more beneath the knife,
>     But having sown prepare to reap;
> Delivered from the crossway rough,
>     Delivered from the thorny scourge,
>     Delivered from the tossing surge,
> Then shall we find—(please God!)—it is enough?
>
> Not in this world of hope deferred,
>     This world of perishable stuff;
> Eye hath not seen, nor ear hath heard,
>     Nor heart conceived that full "enough":
> Here moans the separating sea,
>     Here harvests fail, here breaks the heart;
>     There God shall join and no man part,
> All one in Christ, so one—(please God!)—with me.
>
> (*CP*, 2:267)

In this revised version, more attention is given to God, for in changing "forgetful" to "delivered," Rossetti introduces the Deity as the deliverer. And by adding the parenthetical exclamation "(please God!)," Rossetti adds a note of prayer not part of the original version. Moreover, while this note of prayer has a personal tone, the change Rossetti makes in the last line indicates that the primary theme is not the speaker's redemption but redemption in an all-encompassing sense of the word. In changing "I full of Christ and Christ of me" to "All one in Christ, so one—(please God!)—with me," Rossetti radically alters the meaning. In the revised version, the speaker imagines not a personal relationship with Christ; rather, she imagines merging into the oneness that is Christ, a oneness that includes all the redeemed. In revising "'The Heart Knoweth Its Own Bitterness,'" Rossetti transforms the speaker from one who is focused on his or her own heart's longing for spiritual fulfillment to a speaker who, while still concerned about her own salvation, nevertheless speaks primarily to comfort others. The revised poem is much less focused on self and more focused on the other, that is, on Rossetti's readers. A similar transformation occurs as the result of the revisions Rossetti makes in "Our Heaven," composed in 1854. Since this version can be pieced together only by consulting Crump's endnotes, I shall give it here in full:

> Our heaven must be within ourselves,
> Our only heaven the work of faith,
> Thro' all the race of life that shelves
> Downwards to death.
>
> That calm blue heaven is built too far,
> We cannot reach to hold it fast;
> We cannot touch a single star
> From first to last.
>
> Our powers are strait to compass heaven,
> Our strength is weak to scale the sky;
> There's not one day of all the seven
> That can bring it nigh.
>
> Our heaven must be within our heart,
> Unchangeable for night and day;
> Our heaven must be the better part
> Not taken away.

(2:472)

When Rossetti returns to this early poem and reworks it for inclusion in *Time Flies*, as the reading for November 8, the result is a poem completely different in tone from that version. Whereas that version devotes several lines to describing the physical heaven of the skies, which we cannot reach, the 1885 version offers the reader a joyous vision of a heaven each soul can hope to reach through love. In place of stanzas two through four, Rossetti places the following:

So faith shall build the boundary wall,
 And hope shall plant the secret bower,
 That both may show magnifical
  With gem and flower.

While over all a dome must spread,
 And love shall be that dome above;
 And deep foundations must be laid,
  And these are love.

(2:315)

The note of weariness found in the 1854 version is gone. In this revised version, the reader is reminded of the power of the three Pauline virtues of faith, hope, and love. And Rossetti's imagery of an apocalyptic palace of love underscores Paul's assertion that the greatest of these virtues is love. Again, in the revision process, Rossetti renders an early poem less centered on self and more centered on the other. In the original, the reference to keeping the "better part" calls to mind the image of Mary at the feet of Christ (see Luke 10:42), and thus evokes thoughts of a contemplative life that focuses on the self and her God. By echoing St. Paul, and also the First Epistle of St. John, Rossetti becomes a religious teacher reminding her audience that they must love others if they are to reach the heaven of God's love.

Time Flies offers the reader other poems that echo St. John, such as the poem beginning "'Beloved, let us love one another,'" and the poem beginning "O Ye, who are not dead and fit," which concludes by telling readers to "lead lives of love." However, in The Face of the Deep, the fact that Rossetti is in later life turning to St. John as her guide, and thus turning away from the prophet of Ecclesiastes, becomes even more apparent. Rossetti states in her prefatory note that her sister Maria "pointed out [to her] Patience as our lesson in the Book of Revelations." Yet as one reads through the poems Rossetti includes as part of her commentary on Revelation, it becomes apparent that Rossetti finds a message of love in the visions of St. John, and that divine love is the lesson she offers her readers.

Significantly, early in The Face of the Deep, when commenting on the meaning of Rev. 1:5–6 ("And from Jesus Christ Who is the faithful Witness, and the first begotten of the dead, and the Prince of the kings of the earth. Unto Him that loved us, and washed us from our sins in His own blood, And hath made us kings and priests unto God and His Father: to Him be glory and dominion for ever and ever"), Rossetti indicates that she hears a message of love: "St. John, the Apostle of love, becomes here the mouthpiece of very Love. So that in this Apocalypse not glories only, joys unutterable, perfection, are witnessed to us by Love, but terrors likewise, doom, the Judgment, the opened Books, the lake of fire. Love reveals to us these things, threatens now that it may spare then, shows us destruction lest we destroy ourselves. Let us not in all our tremblings forget or doubt that it is Faithful Love which speaketh" (*FD*, 15). To reinforce this message of love for the reader, Rossetti then places a sonnet that, while echoing several biblical texts, is based primarily upon 1 John 4:7, "God Is Love":

My God, Thyself being Love Thy heart is love,
    And love Thy Will and love Thy Word to us,
    Whether Thou show us depths calamitous
Or heights and flights of rapturous peace above.
O Christ the Lamb, O Holy Ghost the Dove,
    Reveal the Almighty Father unto us;
    That we may tread Thy courts felicitous,
Loving Who loves us, for our God is Love.
Lo, if our God be Love thro' heaven's long day,
    Love is He thro' our mortal pilgrimage,
        Love was He through all aeons that are told.
  We change, but Thou remainest; for Thine age
    Is, Was, and Is to come, nor new nor old;
We change, but Thou remainest; yea and yea!

(CP, 2:235)

Poems on divine love punctuate the volume. For example, when speaking of the patience that is needed "to achieve final perseverance" (*FD*, 75), Rossetti includes a poem on Love:

What is the beginning? Love. What the course? Love still.
What the goal? The goal is Love on the happy hill.
Is there nothing then but Love, search we sky or earth?

There is nothing out of Love hath perpetual worth:
All things flag but only Love, all things fail or flee;
There is nothing left but Love worthy you and me.

(CP, 2:254)

In its use of dialogue and journey motif, this brief lyric, later entitled by Rossetti "'What Hath God Wrought!'" is slightly reminiscent of "Up-Hill." However, in this later lyric, Rossetti comforts the questioning speaker not with a promise of rest but with assurances of divine love. Even Rossetti's lengthy commentary on Rev. 17:1–2, a passage that speaks of the punishment waiting for the "great whore" of Babylon, concludes with a poem on love:

Lord, give me love that I may love Thee much,
    Yea, give me love that I may love Thee more,
    And all for love may worship and adore
And touch Thee with love's consecrated touch.
I halt today; be love my cheerful crutch,
    My feet to plod, some day my wings to soar:
    Some day; but, Lord, not any day before
Thou call me perfect, having made me such.
This is a day of love, a day of sorrow,
    Love tempering sorrow to a sort of bliss;
        A day that shortens while we call it long:
A longer day of love will dawn tomorrow,
    A longer, brighter, lovelier day than this,
        Endless, all love, no sorrow, but a song.

(2:248)

In another of the many poems on love, one placed as part of Rossetti's commentary on Rev. 13:2, is an important reference to "free will" that sheds some light on Rossetti's firm belief both in a God of love and a God of divine justice:

Love is alone the worthy law of love:
    All other laws have presupposed a taint:
    Love is the law from kindled saint to saint,

From lamb to lamb, from dove to answering dove.
Love is the motive of all things that move
  Harmonious by free will without constraint.

(2:220–21)

Rossetti attempted to reconcile her belief in the words of St. John's epistle with his visions of the Last Judgment by turning to the doctrine of free will: "Free will is the foundation of heaven. Free will at the opposite pole is the basis of hell. Free will may not elect hell per se, but by rejecting God it leaves itself no other alternative" (FD, 430). From Rossetti's point of view, it was not so much a loving God who would damn a soul as it was the soul damning itself by refusing God's love. A passage from Seek and Find provides helpful insight into Rossetti's thoughts on the darker passages of Revelation:

> Free will, that one power which God Himself refuses to coerce, free will it is that renders possible our self-destruction [damnation]; and that on the other hand furnishes us with the one solitary thing which as a king we can give unto our all-giving beloved King (see 2 Sam xxiv. 23, 24). Creatures devoid of free-will abide safe and blessed within the will of God; but they cannot withhold, and therefore they cannot genuinely give. Would we, if we could, choose by once for all foregoing choice to offer for ever after unto the Lord our God of that which doth cost us nothing? This were to love mistrustfully, if to love at all: Christ help us to trust entirely because we love much. (186)

For Rossetti, free will, heaven, and hell were all interwoven. If one took away the concept of hell, then one took away free will; and if one took away free will, one took away that which made human beings able to love and therefore made them able to become Christlike.

Not surprisingly, considering Rossetti's repeated echoing of the First Epistle of St. John, one finds in The Face of the Deep that Christ is, at times, spoken of in abstract terms. Although Rossetti still employs the concrete nuptial imagery of the Song of Songs, she also refers to Christ as "the Unbeginning Life" that begins life and "the Endless Life which sustains it [life] endless" (FD, 161). For Rossetti, Christ is still the "Spouse of Souls" (363); yet Christ is also "that true and only and living

166

Centre to which all *living* life gravitates" (288). And, indeed, although the bride and bridegroom imagery of the gospel of Matthew and of the Song of Songs is used throughout Rossetti's commentary on the Apocalypse, she makes it quite clear to her readers that such language is not to be interpreted literally: "For whosoever love God become as chaste virgins espoused to Christ, be they married or single" (138).

As suggested by Rossetti's revision of "'The Heart Knoweth Its Own Bitterness,'" as her understanding of the Deity becomes less anthropomorphic, it also becomes less narrow. By that I mean that she expresses not just a desire to be one with Jesus but also one with all those who love God:

> Lord, make me one with Thine own faithful ones,
>     Thy Saints who love Thee and are loved by Thee;
>     Till the day break and till the shadows flee,
> At one with them in alms and orisons;
> At one with him who toils and him who runs,
>     And him who yearns for union yet to be;
>     At one with all who throng the crystal sea
> And wait the setting of our moons and suns.
> Ah, my beloved ones gone on before,
>     Who looked not back with hand upon the plough!
>         If beautiful to me while still in sight,
>     How beautiful must be your aspects now;
>         Your unknown, well-known aspects in that light
> Which clouds shall never cloud for evermore.

(CP, 2:187–88)

Furthermore, while Rossetti very much believed in individual immortality, as this poem indicates, heaven was not just a place where an individual soul would see those he or she loved in life again, nor was it simply the experience of the individual soul merging with Christ, but a place where all souls form a "communion of lovers":

> The shout of a King is among them. One day may I be
> Of that perfect communion of lovers contented and free
> In the land that is very far off, and far off from the sea.

★

The shout of the King is among them. One King and one
    song,
One thunder of manifold voices harmonious and strong,
One King and one love, and one shout of one worshipping
    throng.

(2:287)

The key word in this poem is simply "one."

A year after *The Face of the Deep* was published, Rossetti's last volume, *Verses*, a collection of the devotional poems previously printed in *Called to Be Saints*, *Time Flies*, and *The Face of the Deep*, appeared. There remains in Rossetti scholarship a tendency to claim that she grew increasingly morbid as she aged.[12] However, these later poems, especially if one reads them all and reads them as they are arranged in *Verses*, simply do not support such a conclusion. In this 1893 volume, Rossetti grouped 331 poems under eight headings: "'Out of the Deep Have I Called Unto Thee, O Lord,'" "Christ Our All in All," "Some Feasts and Fasts," "Gifts and Graces," "The World: Self-Destruction," "Divers Worlds: Time and Eternity," "New Jerusalem and Its Citizens," and "Songs for Strangers and Pilgrims." Though a thorough analysis of all these poems is well beyond the limits of this discussion, even a cursory reading of *Verses* reveals that "love" is a key word throughout.

In "Out of the Deep," the pilgrim voice repeatedly cries out to a God who is identified, in the second poem in this section, as the source of all love: "Thy Love, of each created love the mould" ("Seven vials hold Thy wrath," *CP*, 2:181). In "Christ Our All in All," the reader is repeatedly reminded of Christ's "boundless Love" proven by his crucifixion: "Who shall say 'Nay' when Christ pleads all He is / For us, and holds us with a wounded Hand?" ("Thy Friend and thy Father's Friend forget not," 2:203). "Feasts and Fasts" follows the liturgical calendar and thus includes poems that celebrate the birth of Love [Christ]: "Love came down at Christmas / Love all lovely, Love Divine" ("Christmastide," 2:215). Other poems in this section, those commemorating particular

---

12. See Angela Leighton and Margaret Reynolds, eds., *Victorian Women Poets: An Anthology* (Oxford: Blackwell, 1995), 354.

saints, remind the reader of the loving relationship between Christ and his followers. Significantly, in the penultimate poem in this grouping, "A Song for the Feast of All Saints," Rossetti weaves together saint, speaker, and reader. All are being asked to love Christ:

> As three times to His Saint He saith,
>   He saith to me, He saith to thee,
> Breathing His Grace-conferring Breath:
>   "Lovest thou Me?"
>
> (2:246)

"Gifts and Graces" begins immediately with the focus on love as the primary gift. The first poem begins, "Love Loveth Thee, and wisdom loveth Thee," and moves to the concluding simple sentence, "the whole is love" (2:247). And when Rossetti addresses the subject of grace, again she emphasizes love as all in all: In heaven, "all other graces, to their vast increase / Of glory, look on Love and mirror Love" ("Ye are come unto Mount Sion," 2:259).

*Love* is not a key word in "The World: Self-Destruction," the section in which Rossetti places poems on the end of the world, hell, and damnation; yet even here, one finds a poem asking for God's love in time of judgment: "Be Thy Love before, behind us, / Round us, everywhere" ("'Lord, save us, we perish,'" 2:261). This section, which creates the darkest moment in the whole collection, contains only ten poems, and thus Rossetti does not keep her readers dwelling on thoughts of hell for long. Moreover, "The World: Self-Destruction" is positioned midway in the volume. After the poem beginning "Toll, bell, toll. For hope is flying," Rossetti begins to move the reader, who, after all, still has time to choose God, that is, to choose divine love, to a series of poems in which the speaker is positioned in time but looking to eternity. Although the word *love* does not appear as often in this section as in the first three, eternity is still, nevertheless, defined in terms of divine love: "In that world we weary to attain, / Love's furled banner floats at large unfurled" ("'His Banner over me was Love,'" 2:272). "Divers Worlds" with its emphasis on eternity leads smoothly to "New Jerusalem and Its Citizens," which is defined by Rossetti primarily as a city of love: "And all the trembling there of any string / Is but a trembling of enraptured love" ("When wickedness is broken as a tree," 2:280). Finally, in the last section, echo-ing Heb. 11:13, Rossetti places a variety of poems especially appropriate for her Christian readers, in other words, songs appropriate for those who are not yet citizens of heaven but who have come to realize that they are strangers and pilgrims in this life. Among these various songs, of course, are those that speak of love, such as "O ye, who are not dead and fit," in which the speaker urges the reader to "lead [a] life of love" so that others, seeing such a life, "may kindle too / With love" (CP, 2:312).

With Verses, Rossetti most likely reached a wider audience than she had with the volumes in which the poems were first printed, for as one reviewer noted, Verses "addresses itself definitely to the general public, and can be read without the more or less agreeable interruption of the edifying prose."[13] The reviewers of the time tended to overlook the fact that Verses is, as David A. Kent has shown, a carefully ordered series in which Rossetti traces various stages in the spiritual life as the poet-speaker moves toward an acceptance of God's will.[14] However, as was noted, Rossetti's poetic voice had by her later years changed, and her message was primarily a message of divine love. In his review of Verses, the well-known critic Edmund K. Chambers assessed Rossetti's literary history and concluded, "Love is the keynote of Miss Rossetti's book [Verses]. It is the final outcome of all her disciplines and raptures, her mes-sage, as it was St. John's to her generation."[15]

In September 1894, when Rossetti knew she would soon die of breast cancer, she wrote a note of good-bye to her friend Frederick Shields: "Let us say Good-bye for this life but that is not really for long; let me thank you for your friendship which is precious to me, let me beg your prayers for a poor sinful woman who has dared to speak to others and is herself what God knows her to be. Please remember me very kindly to your wife."[16] Because Rossetti expresses to her friend a desire for his prayers and because she identifies herself as a sinner, some readers might

13. Review of Verses, Athenaeum, December 16, 1893, 842.

14. David A. Kent, "Sequence and Meaning in Rossetti's Verses (1893)," Victorian Poetry 17 (autumn 1979): 259–64. See also Sharon Smulders, Christina Rossetti Revisited (New York: Twayne, 1996), 147–52.

15. Edmund K. Chambers, review of Verses, Academy, February 24, 1894, 163.

16. Quoted in Mary F. Sandars, The Life of Christina Rossetti (London: Hutchinson, 1930), 267.

be inclined to conclude that as Rossetti lay dying, her vision of heaven grew dim.[17] Indeed, if one comes to this letter after reading William Michael Rossetti's description of his sister's last days, a description in which he speaks of her fears of damnation, all one might see in this letter is fear.[18] However, such a reading would be too limited and, perhaps, seriously misguided, for as Kent has recently argued convincingly, to understand "Rossetti's dying" we should view the evidence available within the context of her faith.[19] If we do so, a request that someone pray for her and her view of herself as a sinner need not be read as signs of despair but rather as signs of a devout and humble Christian preparing to die. Furthermore, we should not let Rossetti's experience of dying, whatever it may have been, cloud our reading of her poetry. Ultimately, we cannot know whether in her last moments she felt at peace with her God. What is knowable is that the poetry of her last years (1881–1893) speaks repeatedly not of despair but of belief in the boundless love of God.

Analyses and selections of Rossetti's verse have often concluded with "Sleeping at Last," a poem that leaves the reader with the image of the body resting at peace in the earth, but it is actually far more fitting to choose a poem from the New Jerusalem section of *Verses*. "'Beautiful for situation'" seems especially appropriate:

A lovely city in a lovely land,
    Whose citizens are lovely, and whose King
    Is Very Love; to Whom all Angels sing;
To Whom all saints sing crowned, their scared band
Saluting Love with palm-branch in their hand:
    Thither all doves on gold or silver wing
    Flock home thro' agate windows glistering
Set wide, and where pearl gates wide open stand.
A bower of roses is not half so sweet,

17. For a reading of this letter, which finds in it evidence that Rossetti's vision of heaven "dimmed in her final years," see Antony H. Harrison, *Christina Rossetti in Context* (Chapel Hill: University of North Carolina Press, 1988), 189.

18. For William Michael Rossetti's description of his sister's last days, see *Some Reminiscences*, 2 vols. (1906; rpr., New York: AMS Press, 1970), 2:534–38.

19. David A. Kent, "Christina Rossetti's Dying," *Journal of Pre-Raphaelite Studies*, n.s., 5 (fall 1996): 83–97.

A cave of diamonds doth not glitter so,
  Nor Lebanon is fruitful set thereby:
  And thither thou, beloved, and thither I
May set our heart and set our face and go,
Faint yet pursuing, home on tireless feet.

                                                    (2:283)

When daring to speak to others, Rossetti urged her readers to believe in a never-ending state of love. Certainly, such a belief is neither morbid nor melancholy.

# CONCLUSION
## Secrets

SEVERAL ROSSETTI SCHOLARS HAVE ARGUED THAT WHEN ROS-
setti speaks, she does not tell all; they sense she keeps some secret. As Jan
Marsh notes, biographers "have been intrigued by this baffling sense of
secrecy at the heart of Christina's life, which she was unwilling or unable
to reveal." Critics of Rossetti's poetry have also identified the seemingly
intentional withholding of information as a characteristic of her work.
Taking her title from Rossetti's "Winter: My Secret," Leighton includes
in her analysis of the poet a section entitled "Winter Secrets," in which
she argues that "flaunted secretiveness" often seems to be "the very subject" of Rossetti's poetry." Isobel Armstrong, in her recent study of Victorian poetry, sees "reticence" as characteristic of all Rossetti's verse, and
Armstrong, too, singles out the poem "Winter: My Secret" for special
attention, referring to it as "almost the summa of her [Rossetti's] work."[1]

Twentieth-century Rossetti biographers and critics have been drawn
to this particular poem, perhaps because as a scholar it is easy to imagine
oneself as the unidentified questioner who has asked for the woman's secret and who is not given a simple answer:

1. Jan Marsh, *Christina Rossetti: A Writer's Life* (London: Jonathan Cape, 1994), 99;
Angela Leighton, *Victorian Women Poets: Writing Against the Heart* (Charlottesville: University Press of Virginia, 1992), 155; Isobel Armstrong, *Victorian Poetry: Poetry, Poetic, and Politics* (London: Routledge, 1993), 358.

I tell my secret? No indeed, not I:
Perhaps some day, who knows?
But not today; it froze, and blows, and snows,
And you're too curious: fie!
You want to hear it? well:
Only, my secret's mine, and I won't tell.

Or, after all, perhaps there's none:
Suppose there is no secret after all,
But only just my fun.
Today's a nipping day, a biting day;
In which one wants a shawl,
A veil, a cloak, and other wraps:
I cannot ope to every one who taps,
And let the draughts come whistling thro' my hall;
Come bounding and surrounding me,
Come buffeting, astounding me,
Nipping and clipping thro' my wraps and all.
I wear my mask for warmth: who ever shows
His nose to Russian snows
To be pecked at by every wind that blows?
You would not peck? I thank you for good will,
Believe, but leave that truth untested still.

Spring's an expansive time: yet I don't trust
March with its peck of dust,
Nor April with its rainbow-crowned brief showers,
Nor even May, whose flowers
One frost may wither thro' the sunless hours.

Perhaps some languid summer day,
When drowsy birds sing less and less,
And golden fruit is ripening to excess,
If there's not too much sun nor too much cloud,
And the warm wind is neither still nor loud,
Perhaps my secret I may say,
Or you may guess.

(CP, 1:47)

Biographers have tended to read the "I" of the poem as Rossetti herself and, while noting that the point of this poem may indeed be that there is no secret, have nevertheless more strongly argued that Rossetti is keeping from her readers a very specific secret. Packer, for example, sees in "Winter: My Secret" evidence of Rossetti's supposed love for William Bell Scott. And a more recent biographer, Kathleen Jones also finds a romantic secret; however, she suggests that the poem may offer evidence of "the first stirring of an interest in Cayley." Marsh does not suggest a romantic secret; yet she too appears to see the secret in sexual terms. Finding signs of fear in the poem, she hints at some secret that is too disturbing to be revealed. Because in her biography of the poet, Marsh conjectures that Rossetti was the victim of incest, the implication is that Marsh therefore sees the "winter secret" as sexual abuse.[2]

Other scholars have resisted interpreting the secret in terms of sexuality and have instead read it in terms of autonomy. Instead of focusing on the "secret" in the title, they have focused on the "my." In other words, they claim that keeping silent on some point was for Rossetti a way of achieving independence and even power. For example, Jerome J. McGann reads the secret in this poem as a symbol of "independence and integrity." He concludes, "In the reserve of purpose lies Christina Rossetti's power, her secret, her very self." Frances Thomas reads the poem in somewhat similar terms: "[Rossetti] teases us for the curiosity she knows we feel, incites us almost, but in the end, laughingly claims her right to silence." Leighton and Armstrong also both stress the element of freedom they find in the poem.[3]

In all this guessing of secrets, whether the critic attempts to disclose a definite secret or whether he or she allows Rossetti her privacy, so to speak, scholars have been looking for an explanation. If we either knew what Rossetti's secret was or if we had a suitable gloss for the word *secret,* we would have an approach to her life and poetry that would reveal her

---

2. Lona Mosk Packer, *Christina Rossetti* (Berkeley: University of California Press, 1963), 185; Kathleen Jones, *Learning Not to Be First: The Life of Christina Rossetti* (Gloucestershire: Windrush Press, 1991), 109; Marsh, *Christina Rossetti,* 198–99.

3. Jerome J. McGann, "Christina Rossetti's Poems: A New Edition and a Revaluation," *Victorian Studies,* 23 (winter 1980): 246–47; Frances Thomas, *Christina Rossetti* (Hanley Swan, Eng.: Self-Publishing Association, 1992), 149; Leighton, *Victorian Women Poets,* 154; and Armstrong, *Victorian Poetry,* 358.

to us; that is, it would explain her and the work. In fact, this "guessing" at winter secrets serves to represent scholarship on Rossetti. By the time of Rossetti's death, Victorians tended to see faith as her secret. (Even this seemingly playful poem could easily be read as in keeping with Rossetti's belief that only in heaven would all secrets be revealed.) Later readers, especially those influenced by psychoanalytic theory, have decided that sex or at least sexual repression is the secret. Those who thought Rossetti's verse merely pretty, all sound and little sense, appear to have concluded she had no secret worth guessing at. Those of the 1980s onward seem inclined to find in Rossetti's perceived secrecy an independence of spirit, and such a reading certainly owes something to the recent influence of feminist theories and the resulting movement to find strong-minded women writers to include in the canon.

In guessing Rossetti's secret, the focus has tended to be on a single secret—romantic, sexual, spiritual, or political—which, if we could name it, would explain all her poetry. Such an approach has its dangers, for it implies that there is only one major secret that influenced her work and only one manner in which Rossetti responded to that influence. Such an approach can easily lead to an image of Rossetti that is one-dimensional. Rossetti was a complex woman who certainly had more than one secret. Moreover, attempting to uncover only one secret often does not allow Rossetti to be a poet; in other words, it does not allow for the power of her imagination or even for her desire not to be silent but to speak to others. Indeed, one might argue that the secret in "Winter: My Secret" is that Rossetti took pleasure in creating poetry that others would read; and thus, this particular winter secret is actually revealed to us, for it is the poem itself. Yet such a reading is also too reductive, suggesting again that a single answer can be found.

When we attempt to decipher the poet's secret in "Winter: My Secret" and in all Rossetti's poems, it is far more useful to think in terms of secrets, that is, in terms of the complexity of the woman who wrote the poems. Although Rossetti became, at a young age, a devout Christian, that faith was not static, and it did not isolate her from the world. Rather, it led her to respond in complex ways to the world of Victorian society. And often her response was strongly shaped not only by her faith but by her experience of having been born female. Clearly, her poems speak of what we might consider women's issues—religious sisterhoods, prostitution, illegitimacy, marriage, and suffrage. Yet her poetic voice was not and is not just for women. And it is important to remember that during the last decades of her life, she is writing repeatedly of a spiritual world where gender has no meaning, where male and female are one. My aim has been to show that among her secrets were Rossetti's faith, her gender, and the times in which she was a woman of faith. All should be considered when scholarly curiosity leads us to ask this poet for her secrets.

# SELECTED BIBLIOGRAPHY

Addison, Jane. "Christina Rossetti Studies, 1974–1991: A Checklist and Synthesis." *Bulletin of Bibliography* 2 (March 1995): 73–93.

Arseneau, Mary. "Incarnation and Interpretation: Christina Rossetti, and the Oxford Movement, and 'Goblin Market.'" *Victorian Poetry* 31 (1993): 79–93.

———. "Pilgrimage and Postponement: Christina Rossetti's 'The Prince's Progress.'" *Victorian Poetry* 32 (autumn–winter 1994): 279–98.

Battiscombe, Georgina. *Christina Rossetti: A Divided Life*. London: Constable, 1981.

Bell, Mackenzie. *Christina Rossetti: A Biographical and Critical Study*. Boston: Roberts Brothers, 1898.

Blake, Kathleen. *Love and the Woman Question in Victorian Literature: The Art of Self-Postponement*. Totowa, N.J.: Barnes and Noble, 1983.

Casey, Janet Galligani. "The Potential of Sisterhood: Christina Rossetti's 'Goblin Market.'" *Victorian Poetry* 29 (spring 1991): 63–78.

Crump, Rebecca W. *Christina Rossetti: A Reference Guide*. Boston: G. K. Hall, 1976.

Festa, Conrad. "Renunciation in Christina Rossetti's Poetry." *Pre-Raphaelite Review* 3 (May 1980): 25–35.

Henwood, Dawn. "Christian Allegory and Subversive Poetics: Christina Rossetti's *Prince's Progress* Reexamined." *Victorian Poetry* 35 (1997): 83–94.

Harrison, Antony H. *Christina Rossetti in Context*. Chapel Hill: University of North Carolina Press, 1988.

———. "Christina Rossetti and the Sage Discourse of Feminist High Anglicanism." In *Victorian Sages and Cultural Discourse: Renegotiating Gender and Power*, ed. Thais E. Morgan, 87–104. New Brunswick, N.J.: Rutgers University Press, 1990.

———, ed. *The Collected Letters of Christina Rossetti*. 4 vols. Charlottesville: University Press of Virginia, 1997–.

Hickok, Kathleen. *Representations of Women: Nineteenth-Century British Women's Poetry*. Westport, Conn.: Greenwood Press, 1984.

Hobbs, Colleen. "A View from 'The Lowest Place': Christina Rossetti's Devotional Prose." *Victorian Poetry* 32 (autumn–winter 1994): 409–28.

Honnighausen, Gisela. "Emblematic Tendencies in the Works of Christina Rossetti." *Victorian Poetry* 10 (1972): 1–15.

Jimenez, Nilda. *The Bible and the Poetry of Christina Rossetti: A Concordance*. Westport, Conn.: Greenwood Press, 1979.

Jones, Kathleen. *Learning Not to Be First: The Life of Christina Rossetti*. Gloucestershire: Windrush, 1991.

Kent, David A., ed. *The Achievement of Christina Rossetti*. Ithaca: Cornell University Press, 1987.

———. "Christina Rossetti's Dying." *Journal of Pre-Raphaelite Studies*, n.s., 5 (fall 1996): 83–97.

———. "Sequence and Meaning in Rossetti's *Verses* (1893)." *Victorian Poetry* 17 (autumn 1979): 259–64.

Leder, Sharon, with Andrea Abbott. *The Language of Exclusion: The Poetry of Emily Dickinson and Christina Rossetti*. Westport, Conn.: Greenwood Press, 1987.

Leighton, Angela. *Victorian Women Poets: Writing Against the Heart*. Charlottesville: University Press of Virginia, 1992.

Marsh, Jan. *Christina Rossetti: A Writer's Life*. London: Jonathan Cape, 1994.

Marshall, Linda E. " 'Transfigured to His Likeness': Sensible Transcendentalism in Christina Rossetti's 'Goblin Market.' " *University of Toronto Quarterly* 63 (spring 1994): 429–50.

———. "What the Dead Are Doing Underground: Hades and Heaven in the Writings of Christina Rossetti." *Victorian Newsletter* 72 (1987): 55–60.

McGann, Jerome J. "Christina Rossetti's Poems: A New Edition and a Revaluation." *Victorian Studies* 23 (winter 1980): 237–54.

———. "The Religious Poetry of Christina Rossetti." *Critical Inquiry* 10 (1983): 127–43.

Mayberry, Katherine J. *Christina Rossetti and the Poetry of Discovery*. Baton Rouge: Louisiana State University Press, 1989.

Mermin, Dorothy. "Heroic Sisterhood in *Goblin Market*." *Victorian Poetry* 21 (1983): 107–18.

Morrison, Ronald D. " 'One droned in sweetness like a fattened bee': Christina Rossetti's View of Marriage in Her Early Poetry." *Kentucky Philological Review* 5 (1990): 19–26.

Nockles, Peter Benedict. *The Oxford Movement in Context: Anglican High Churchmanship, 1760–1857*. Cambridge: Cambridge University Press, 1994.

Palazzo, Lynda. "The Prose Works of Christina Rossetti." Ph.D. diss., University of Durham, Eng., 1992.

Packer, Lona Mosk. *Christina Rossetti*. Berkeley: University of California Press, 1963.

Peterson, Linda. "Restoring the Book: The Typological Hermeneutics of Christina Rossetti and the PRB." *Victorian Poetry* 32 (autumn–winter 1994): 209–27.

Rees, Joan. "Christina Rossetti: Poet." *Critical Quarterly* 26 (autumn 1984): 59–72.

Rosenblum, Dolores. *Christina Rossetti: The Poetry of Endurance*. (Carbondale, Ill.: Southern Illinois University Press, 1986).

Rossetti, Christina. *Annus Domini: A Prayer for Each Day of the Year, Founded on a Text of Holy Scripture*. Oxford: James Parker, 1874.

———. *Called to Be Saints: The Minor Festivals Devotionally Studied*. London: Society for Promoting Christian Knowledge, 1881.

———. *Letter and Spirit: Notes on the Commandments*. London: Society for Promoting Christian Knowledge, 1883.

———. *Maude: Prose and Verse*. Edited by R. W. Crump. Hamden, Conn.: Archon Books, 1976.

———. *Time Flies: A Reading Diary*. London: Society for Promoting Christian Knowledge, 1885.

———. *The Face of the Deep: A Devotional Commentary on the Apocalypse*. London: Society for Promoting Christian Knowledge, 1892.

———. *The Complete Poems of Christina Rossetti*. Edited by Rebecca W. Crump. 3 vols. Baton Rouge: Louisiana State University Press, 1979, 1986, 1990.

Rossetti, William Michael, ed. *The Poetical Works of Christina Georgina Rossetti*. London: Macmillan, 1904.

Schofield, Linda. "Displaced and Absent Texts as Contexts for Christina Rossetti's *Monna Innominata*." *Journal of Pre-Raphaelite Studies* 6 (spring 1997): 38–52.

Shalkhauser, Marian. "The Feminine Christ." *Victorian Newsletter* 10 (autumn 1956): 19–20.

Sickbert, Virgina. "'Beloved Mother of Us All': Christina Rossetti's Eve." *Christianity and Literature* 44 (April 1995): 289–312.

Smulders, Sharon. *Christina Rossetti Revisited*. New York: Twayne, 1996.

Tennyson, G. B. *Victorian Devotional Poetry: The Tractarian Mode*. Cambridge: Harvard University Press, 1981.

Thomas, Frances. *Christina Rossetti*. Hanley Swan, Eng.: Self-Publishing Association, 1992.

Waller, John O. "Christ's Second Coming: Christina Rossetti and the Premillennialist William Dodsworth." *Bulletin of the New York Public Library* 73 (1969): 465–82.

Westerholm, Joel. "'I Magnify Mine Office': Christina Rossetti's Authoritative Voice in Her Devotional Prose." *Victorian Newsletter* 84 (1993): 11–17.

# INDEX

mother, 120, 126, 129; in Rossetti's
"Eve," 120–24; in Browning's
"Drama of Exile," 122, 135–38; in
Gessner's *Death of Abel*, 122; Satan's
temptation of, 123–26, 128; and
life, not death, 124–25; in Rossetti's
"Afterthought," 124, 127; Paul on,
127; as wife, 127; Victorian interest
in, and woman question, 129–30
Evil. *See* Satan; Sin
"Eye Hath Not Seen," 70

*Face of the Deep*, 53, 63, 66, 75, 76, 78,
79, 80, 86–87, 98, 113, 116, 119–20,
123, 128, 133, 138, 139–40, 142,
146, 148, 149, 152–53, 157, 160,
163–68
Faith: Victorian view of Rossetti's
faith, 1, 2–3, 4, 5, 15–16; twentieth-
century prefeminist view of Rossetti's faith, 3–7, 11–12; feminist views
of Rossetti's faith, 89, 61; and
"Heart Knoweth Its Own Bitterness," 13–17; as Rossetti's response
to feminine voice of woe, 23–42;
and vanity of earthly things, 25–27,
49, 50, 62–64; and religious verse by
women poets in early nineteenth
century, 27–36; and Bible study by
Rossetti, 30; and eschatology, 34–
36, 40–41, 53–54; in *Maude*, 37–40;
and renunciation, 45, 61–66; and
"Goblin Market," 69–83; and baptism, 79–80; in Incarnation, 79;
Rossetti's faith learned from
mother, 143–44; and religious
doubt during Victorian Age,
147–48; and Rossetti's creativity,
148–49; in Rossetti's later poetry,
149–72; and gloomy Christians,

156–57; and responsibilities of
Christian to others, 157–63; and
sorrow transformed into joy,
157–63; and free will, 165–66. *See
also* Biblical allusions; Christ;
Heaven
Fallen women: in Rossetti's convent
poems, 49, 50, 51, 52, 55; in nineteenth-century poetry generally, 67,
94, 95–96, 97, 99, 103; in "Goblin
Market," 72, 108; in "Apple-Gathering," 94, 99, 101–102, 109; in
"Cousin Kate," 94, 99, 100, 102,
109, 110; and illegitimate children,
94, 96–97, 109–13; in "Iniquity of
the Fathers Upon the Children,"
94, 99, 109–13; in "Light Love,"
94, 95–100, 102, 109, 110; in "Margery," 94, 99, 100–101, 102, 109,
113–14; compared with virgin
bride, 97–100, 109; and condemnation of fallen men, 98–99, 109, 111;
Victorian view of, 102–109; at
Highgate penitentiary, 104–109,
113n15; and Mary Magdalene, 115–
17. *See also* Eve
"Feast of the Annunciation," 134
Feminist interpretations, 7–9, 12–13,
16, 61, 176
"First Spring Day," 55
Fletcher, C. J. H., 133–34
Flower imagery, 31–32, 51, 74–75, 87,
89
"Flowers Appear on the Earth,"
72–73
"Fluttered Wings," 150
Free will, 165–66
Freudian interpretations. *See* Psycho-
analytic interpretations
"From House to Home," 64
Fullerton, Georgina, 20, 24–25